The Manchurian Candidate, Part 1,
Putin Plays His Trump Card.

by Paul Covell, © 2017 by Paul Covell
All Rights Reserved
CreateSpace Edition

Table of Contents

Foreword

This story relates facts concerning some of the events of the 2015-2016 presidential campaign and interference by hackers working for Russia. There is a suggestion of a fantasy of mind control not based on facts. Known facts are that candidate Donald J. Trump hired Paul Manafort Campaign Manager and Lt. Gen. (Ret.) Michael Flynn Security Adviser in 2016. In 2017, Manafort and Flynn registered after the fact as Foreign Agents. Manafort took money for advice given from 2010-2014 to Viktor Yanukovych, President of Ukraine, a surrogate for Vladimir Putin, President of Russia. Flynn's company accepted payments in 2015 from Russia and Turkey without Pentagon permission.

What is fantasy is the suggestion that President Trump is or would be an agent of Russia. There is no evidence that candidate Trump ever underwent any mind control or hypnosis that would leave him vulnerable to post hypnotic suggestion. Russia may have something on President Trump or on his 2016 Campaign that could affect Trump's freedom of choice. FBI surveillance showed that the Russians compromised Lt. Gen (Ret.) Michael Flynn. Russians call it *'Kompromat'* Flynn compromised himself by informing Vice President Pence that he did not discuss sanctions with the Russians. President Trump dismissed Flynn as a security risk.

Vladimir Putin chafed at the breakup of the Soviet Union. He could not accept what he considered the betrayal by Mikhail Gorbachev and Boris Yeltsin. Together, they ceded Russia's influence to the U.S. and the West. At least Yeltsin, appointed Putin to the caretaker post of a Deputy Premier of the Soviet Union. Yeltsin agreed to the downsizing of the USSR, and resigned in 1999. Putin seized control of a slimmed down Russia, and, as his first decree, granted Yeltsin immunity from prosecution. A remarkable rise to power by a former KGB Colonel.

He resolved to restore power to Russia at the expense of the U.S. He faced two existential challenges. The Russian Navy had no homeport. NATO forces hemmed in the Army. Ukraine won independence from the Soviet Union in 1991. Crimea and the large naval base at Sevastopol went with Ukraine, which had been under Russian governance since Catherine the Great annexed the territory in 1883. Putin was fighting mad, but he preferred cyberwar to nuclear confrontation.

Donald Trump is a real estate developer, who as President wants to remake America in his image. He always looked for challenges for stimulation and profit. His father, Fred Trump, built middle-income apartments in Queens and Brooklyn, New York. Fred stayed away from development in Manhattan, because of the increased cost and risk involved. Donald could not wait to make it in Manhattan. As a teenager, Donald slipped into Manhattan a number of times against his father's rules. To instill discipline, Fred sent Donald to school at New York Military Academy sixty miles north of New York City. Trump graduated, spent two years at Fordham, and reportedly earned a bachelor's degree in real estate or finance during two years at University of Pennsylvania. Trump received deferments from the draft as a student.

After graduation, Trump's doctor diagnosed bone spurs on the heel, earning Trump a medical disqualification from military service. He feels his experience at New York Military Academy was all the military experience he needed. Trump joined the family business, took on projects in Manhattan, and constructed Trump Tower at 725 Fifth Avenue.

In *The Manchurian Candidate* 1962 film, Lawrence Harvey and Frank Sinatra appeared as members of an American Army infantry platoon engaged in a firefight in the Korean War. A Russian Airborne Unit captured them, flew them to Manchuria, and, with the help of the Chinese, subjected them to post hypnotic mind control. Ironically, Harvey's mother, played by Angela Lansbury, was Harvey's *U.S. operator*. The key to triggering Harvey into a robotic trance was the *Queen of Diamonds.* Lansbury's husband in the film sought the vice presidency. Lansbury's mission was to program Harvey to assassinate the presidential candidate to allow her husband to fill in as the presidential candidate.

Lansbury first had to deal with a Senator Jordan, who vowed to block Lansbury's husband from winning the nomination as Vice President. Harvey had a crush on the Senator's daughter. Lansbury invited the Senator and daughter to a costume party to win over the Senator. The daughter arrived dressed as the *Queen of Diamonds*. Harvey and the daughter elope. The Senator tells Lansbury he is adamantly opposed to her husband. Lansbury orders Harvey to shoot the Senator. Harvey also shot the daughter, Harvey's new wife, who was visiting her father.

Captain Frank Sinatra, working with Army intelligence, tries to deprogram Harvey with a deck of fifty-two Queens of Diamonds. Sinatra learns by a telephone call from Harvey that the mission is to shoot the presidential candidate at the convention during the acceptance speech. Sinatra races to the convention to try to stop Harvey. Arriving too late, Sinatra sees that Harvey shot Lansbury and her husband instead of the target Lansbury ordered.

In real life, the U.S. Government became alarmed at the advances in psychological conditioning and mind control made by the Chinese and Russians during the Korean War. CIA developed U.S. psychological conditioning techniques in response.

Conspiracy Theory, 1997 film with Mel Gibson, Julia Roberts, and Patrick Stewart, recalls CIA's MKUltra Project involving mind control. Jerry Fletcher (Gibson) drives a taxi in New York. He sees conspiracies everywhere. Alice Sutton (Roberts) is an Assistant U.S. Attorney. She tolerates his eccentricities because he saved her from a mugging. CIA psychiatrist Dr. Jonas (Stewart) searches for Jerry because Jerry is a survivor of the Ultra Project and proof of CIA experimentation with drugs to control minds of subjects. CIA programmed Jerry years ago as an assassin to shoot a judge, who was Alice's father. Jerry resisted the order, and vowed to watch over Alice. Another assassin killed her father. Dr. Jonas captures Jerry, who knows too much about the Project, and tortures him. Alice came in with the FBI and rescued Jerry.

CIA could not hide MKUltra because of the size and scope of the Project. The program consisted of 149 subprojects contracted out to 80 universities and research foundations. In response to the Government's denial of a Freedom of Information Request, the U.S. Supreme Court upheld secrecy for CIA's sources and methods. *CIA v. Sims*, (1985) 471 U.S. 159. CIA devised MKUltra to counter Soviet and Chinese advances in brainwashing and interrogation techniques.

President Trump disagrees that seventeen U.S. intelligence agencies found Russian interference with the 2016 presidential election. He infers that the main impetus for finding Russian interference comes from CIA and FBI. He fired FBI Director James B. Comey on May 9, 2017.He dismisses CIA capability because of mistaken finding of Weapon of Mass Destruction in Iraq as justification for the 2003 invasion ordered by President George W. Bush.

President Trump refuses to take a firm stand on Russian interference. He says it may have been Russia or other countries. To that extent, he makes it easier for Vladimir Putin to deny Russian involvement. Former FBI Director Robert Mueller is Special Counsel to investigate the matter. Trump and adviser Roger Stone urged Russia and WikiLeaks to release Hillary emails.

Special Counsel Mueller may not look for hypnotic suggestion to explain the President's bias toward Russia. He will be looking for blackmail. The Russians call it *'Kompromat'*, Compromising Materials. Trump had to fire Lt. Gen. (Ret.) Michael Flynn as National Security Adviser, because the Russians knew Flynn lied when he misstated for the record that he did not discuss sanctions with Russian Ambassador Sergey Kislyak. After Team Trump denied for a year colluding with the Russians, on July 11, 2017, Donald Trump, Jr. admitted taking a meeting with Natalia Veselnitskaya, an attorney close to the Kremlin, for the express purpose of receiving incriminating evidence about Hillary Clinton from Russia's state prosecutor.

Donald Trump, Jr. released the email chain that documented the purpose of the meeting he attended along with Campaign Manager, Paul Manafort, and brother in law, Jared Kushner. The President praised his son for *transparency* for releasing the email chain one hour before promised release by the New York Times. The Nation will remain in jeopardy until we learn what the Russians have on the President to compromise his behavior in office. *It all goes back to Trump's financial struggles and the Miss Universe Contest that Trump brought to Moscow in 2013.*

<u>Chapter 1</u>

Stunning Surprise for Hillary Clinton on November 8, 2016.

Viktor Yanukovych, elected President of Ukraine in 2010, after an ongoing east-west struggle, made a fateful decision, and chose closer affiliation with Russia over joining the European Union. Vladimir Putin, President of Russia, continued to salvage what was left of the Russian Navy after the dissolution of the USSR. Paul Manafort, an American lawyer and lobbyist, was political adviser to Yanukovych. In 2014, Ukrainian patriots overthrew the Yanukovych regime. As a counter to his loss of influence over Ukraine, wielded through Yanukovych, Putin invaded Crimea. To maintain land access to Sevastopol, he sent Russian troops, *without unit insignia*, to destabilize Eastern Ukraine.

Anatoly Antonov, Deputy Defense Minister, supervised Russian destabilization of eastern Ukraine. European Union will not grant diplomatic status to Antonov. Putin made a masterstroke move, while President Trump distracted himself from emergent duties of office and wasted time by fretting over the crowd size at his Inauguration. Putin wanted to remove Ambassador Kislyak from U.S. questioning with respect to Russian interference in the U.S. 2016 presidential election. Putin recalled Kislyak, and replaced him with Antonov. There was not even a whimper from the Administration, which has yet to admit that the Russians hacked into the computers of Democratic National Committee (DNC) and John Podesta, Campaign Manager for Hillary Clinton.

President Obama imposed economic sanctions on Russia but did not press military action, because Ukraine was not a NATO Member. President Trump, from the outset, favored lifting sanctions against Russia *without requiring any change in behavior by Russia*. His bias toward Russia is not normal for a U.S. president. Until the mystery of Russian influence over Trump solves, nothing can be done in Washington.

Putin claims patriots rose up against harsh rule of despots in Kiev who were running eastern Ukraine Those patriots spoke Russian and acted as though they were in the military, despite the fact that they had no shoulder patches to identify their units.

Russia's State Security Service, FSB, formerly known as KGB, developed computer hacking techniques to subvert Western Democracies politically by manipulating the outcome of elections. It was easier for Russia to fight the battle by corrupting ballots rather than shooting bullets. Why not combine computer hacking with disinformation, propaganda, and bullying to stop the election of strong democratic candidates who would oppose Russia?

Hillary Clinton looked like the choice of the Democrats in 2015. If elected, she would be a determined foe of Russia. On the Republican side, Donald Trump appeared to be the best choice for Russia. He was not an ideologue. Trump was a businessperson, who wanted to build hotels, office buildings, and golf courses. More than one Russian billionaire oligarch expressed an interest in investing in the Trump Organization. Putin was fascinated with the vagaries of American politics. Hillary was vulnerable because of the investigation of the 2012 terrorist attack on the U.S. Diplomatic Mission at Benghazi, Libya, an attack for which she was not to blame. The CIA controlled most of the diplomatic post. Congress cut the budget for security for State Department.

The other political attack on Hillary stemmed from the FBI Investigation over email security procedures during her tenure as Secretary of State. State Department Inspector General allowed Hillary to maintain a private server at home. After Hillary left State, the Inspector General investigated her use of a home server, and sent a Report to Justice Department. The FBI conducted a two-year investigation that spanned the primary and general elections of 2105-2106. Putin could not have been more pleased if he had written the script. He did not want to deal with a President Clinton. He could not imagine how email procedures could bring down a Russian Leader, but he would help disrupt America if he could. America was asleep.

Putin talked with his former KGB colleagues, now working at FSB State Security. They knew about Julius Assange, his gripe with Hillary Clinton, and the WikiLeaks portal. They also knew that the computers in the offices of the Democratic National Committee (DNC) and John Podesta, Hillary's Campaign Manager, would be soft targets for FSB Hackers. If emails could be firecrackers for Republicans to throw at the Hillary Clinton Campaign, FSB hackers came up with thousands of emails related to Hillary Clinton. WikiLeaks released the emails to the public.

The propaganda campaign began to take its toll on Hillary's poll numbers. FBI Director, James B. Comey, delivered a twin coup de grace by announcing in July 2016 that the Justice Department would not prosecute Hillary Clinton *despite the sloppiness* of her email security, and by announcing eleven days before the election that the FBI *re-opened* the Investigation to examine another batch of Hillary emails. After the Election, Trump rewarded Comey by firing him for not backing off the investigation into Russian interference in the 2016 election.

The Russians played Team Trump for amateurs and fools. Alternatively, Trump is playing the American People for fools. Trump and son in law Jared Kushner cannot serve the Nation because of irreconcilable conflicts of interest from their business interests, and from possible Russian investments in the Trump Organization. From 2010 to 2014, Trump interim Campaign Manager Paul Manafort advised Putin puppet Viktor Yanukovych President of Ukraine. General

Michael Flynn's company accepted $45,000 from *Russia Today*, a Russian Government propaganda outlet, and attended a banquet in Russia with Vladimir Putin sitting at the same table.

Flynn's company accepted $450,000 from Turkey, and those funds may have a Russian connection as well. Flynn may have violated U.S. law if he did not have permission of the Defense Department to take payments from sources connected with foreign governments. Secretary of State Rex Tillerson, former Head of Exxon Mobil, has dined with Putin in Moscow. Putin awarded him the *Order of Friendship Medal*, formerly known as the *Order of Lenin*, for negotiating a major contract between Russia's Rosneft Oil Company and Exxon Mobil to develop petroleum resources in Russia.

Trump Campaign consultant Carter Page made several trips to Moscow. As result of sanctions imposed by President Obama, the contract between Exxon and Russian State Oil Company Rosneft is on hold. The contract could have a sales value to Exxon in the range of up to several billions of dollars. If Trump and Tillerson arrange to lift the sanctions against Russia, the Exxon Russia contract could go forward. Michael Flynn spoke multiple times by telephone with Russian Ambassador Sergey Kislyak. *As Security Adviser to the U.S., Flynn assured Vice President Pence that he did not discuss the sanctions President Obama imposed on Russia for invading Crimea and eastern Ukraine.* Pence publicized Flynn's denial, and thus made Flynn's story part of the public record. FBI transcripts of the telephone conversations apparently showed that Flynn discussed sanctions.

Acting Attorney General Sally Yates, an Obama holdover, informed Trump White House Counsel Don McGahn that Flynn was at risk of blackmail by Russia because of lying about discussion of sanctions. Trump dismissed Flynn twenty-four days later for misinforming the Vice President about discussing sanctions with the Russians. Attorney General Sessions recused himself from the investigation of Russian interference and possible collusion of the Trump Campaign with the Russians, because Sessions was a surrogate for Trump during the Campaign. Deputy Attorney General Rod Rosenstein made decisions for the Justice Department on the Russian investigation until appointment of Special Counsel Robert Mueller.

Trump disdained the Russian investigation as an attempt by Democrats to reverse the 2016 election. Trump had private discussions with FBI Head James B. Comey. The FBI Director wrote memos to the file documenting that Trump asked Comey if he could let go of the investigation of Flynn.

Trump dismissed Comey on May 9, 2017, purportedly on recommendation of Deputy Attorney General Rod Rosenstein. Rosenstein stated that he knew Trump decided to remove the FBI Director before Rosenstein wrote his recommendation. Trump denied that he tried to influence Comey to drop the Flynn investigation, and floated a warning that Comey *'better make sure there is no tape'* of the dinner conversation before Comey leaks to the press. Multiple Committees in Congress demand to see Comey's memos to the file and any tape of the dinner conversation with Comey. To assure public confidence in the integrity of the investigation of the Russian Connection, Deputy Attorney General Rod Rosenstein appointed former FBI Director Robert Mueller as Special Counsel to head the Russian Investigation.

Jared Kushner may have discussed refinancing the $1.2 billion mortgage on his company's property at 666 Fifth Avenue with Russian Ambassador Sergey Kislyak. Kislyak reportedly referred Kushner to VEB Russia State Bank and billionaire Sergey Gorkov. Russia owns VEB Bank, and the bank's Chairman must be the Premier of Russia. Gorkov is a graduate of the Spy School run by FSB (State Security Service), successor to Russia's KGB. Russian President Putin, a former KGB Colonel, must be amazed and pleased at the naiveté of Kushner, Flynn, and Trump. After winning the election, Trump apparently sent Kushner to explore setting up a back channel using Russian diplomatic facilities and Russian communications equipment. Trump did not trust the U.S. Government, and apparently trusted the Russian Government.

Everyone was surprised, some shocked, when Donald Trump beat Hillary Clinton on November 8, 2016. The election was Hillary's to lose, and the same caution, concern for personal finances, and deference to institutions that haunted Hillary over the years—and tethered her from reaching her full potential—resulted in the loss to Trump. Of course, there were outside countervailing forces. FBI Director James B. Comey held a press conference in July 5, 2016, to announce that there would be no prosecution of Clinton for mishandling State Department emails on her home server. Comey violated Justice Department policy when he went on to criticize Clinton for *'sloppiness'* in her email security. When the Government prosecutes, the accusation itself necessarily embodies derogatory allegations.

When the government at any level decides not prosecute, the FBI or Justice Department or state prosecutors cannot lawfully publish derogatory information about the target in a misguided effort to balance the equities between political parties or for any other reason. Comey felt political pressure because many Officials and Agents in the FBI, as well as many Republicans, favored prosecution of Clinton.

As a former U.S. Attorney and Acting Attorney General, Comey felt confident as FBI Chief to announce a decision not to prosecute Hillary Clinton. Justice Department decides prosecutions, however, not the FBI. Comey acted outside his lane, which Trump's Deputy Attorney General Rod Rosenstein used to justify Comey's dismissal. Former Attorney General Lynch recused herself from involvement in the Clinton investigation after Bill Clinton barged in on her *to chat about grandchildren* while they both were on planes stopped at the same airport. The Lynch recusal opened the door for a Comey Press Conference. Comey's announcement not to prosecute Obama's favorite to succeed him no doubt met President Obama's approval.

It is bizarre that President Trump fired Comey on May 9, 2017, on the pretext of Comey's mishandling the Clinton investigation. It was the FBI probe into possible collusion between the Russians and the Trump Campaign, however, which weighed heavily on Trump.

Comey's last bombshell for Clinton eleven days before the election announced that the FBI *re-opened* the investigation to review another batch of newly found Clinton emails. A few days later, Comey announced that no new issues developed from the new emails. Comey's on-again-off-again FBI investigation of Clinton raised doubts about Clinton.

Hillary, however, lost the election on her own. Hillary and her advisers were vulnerable because they believed their own talking points and the hyped projection of election results based upon polls. Most national polls showed Hillary winning the 2016 election by 2½ percent of the vote. *The* virtual *Blue Wall* of presumed Democratic pluralities in Wisconsin, Michigan, and Pennsylvania supposedly would keep Candidate Trump out of the White House. It was conventional wisdom in the media—with the notable exception of Rupert Murdoch's Fox News, Wall Street Journal, and Washington Times—that there was *no path* of state victories by which Trump could reach 270, a majority of Electoral Votes needed to win. By mid-evening on November 8, it became obvious that the National Polls would not save Hillary. *Election results had to tally state by state.*

Trump shattered the virtual *Blue Wall*, and carried Wisconsin, Michigan, and Pennsylvania. Hillary won the popular vote by about 2½ points, or nearly three million votes. Trump won the Presidency by taking 304 Electoral Votes.

Hillary's Mistakes.

Throughout the Campaign, Hillary never appeared in Wisconsin, taking the progressive state for granted. She had little to say about bringing back American jobs, especially in manufacturing. *By default, Hillary allowed the Republican billionaire candidate to play the populist, and champion the cause of the American worker.* Trump turned the tables on Clinton and the Democrats, who blissfully accepted their fate as Washington and East Coast Elites. Hillary's overweening caution undermined her chances to win. She was determined to make the safest pick for Vice President, and not make any waves. Hillary feared to run with progressive fire-brands like Senators Bernie Sanders and Elizabeth Warren, both of whom would counter Trump's claim to be the only populist in the race. Hillary chose Virginia Senator Tim Kaine as the least risky bet.

To make matters worse, Hillary's team may have prepped Kaine to interrupt Mike Pence repeatedly to make the Vice President candidates' debate edgy, and knock Pence off stride. The more Kaine interrupted, the more Pence scored points. Since the time of the Bill Clinton (Arkansas) and Al Gore (Tennessee) ticket in 1992-2000, presidential candidates wrongly assumed geographic balance was not essential.

Clinton Kaine, however, was the model for an East Coast Elitist Ticket. Hillary ignored the Rust Belt and the American worker at her peril. Did the Democrats consider selecting Jennifer Granholm for Vice President? As former Governor of Michigan, Granholm could have made a positive difference in Wisconsin, Michigan, and Pennsylvania, the states that cost Hillary the election. Trump won Wisconsin by 22,748, votes, Michigan by 10,704 votes, and Pennsylvania by 46,765 votes. Democrats would have done better with Ohio Senator Sherrod Brown. Hillary's fear of defying political and social custom likely prevented selection of Granholm or Warren. She feared it would be too much to have two women on the ticket. Hillary talked about breaking up the banks. She accepted $600,000 from Goldman Sachs for a speech, and refused to disclose the text of her talk.

The Clinton campaign was awash in Campaign contributions. Hillary did not need to take money from Wall Street, which the Democratic Base blamed for the 2008 Recession and millions of lost jobs and mortgage defaults.

The email fiasco was a mess created entirely by Hillary Clinton, Bill Clinton, and their advisers. She wanted to keep her private emails confidential, as would anyone. However, the answer was not to put State Department emails at risk by using a home server. *If a hacker breaks into a State Department server, the responsibility for security and any breach is on the Government.* Hillary was at risk for anything that might happen through use of the Clintons' home server. She should have used the State Department email system for State Department emails.

The State Department Inspector General was negligent in not forcing the Secretary of State to use the Government server from the start.

After Clinton resigned, the State Department Inspector General investigated Hillary's use of the home server, and referred the findings to the FBI for possible prosecution. *Hillary needlessly burdened her Campaign with a two-year FBI Investigation, and opened the door to GOP carping, 'Lock her up, Lock her up.'*

Russian Interference.

Seventeen U.S. intelligence agencies concluded that Russia interfered, and tried to influence the outcome of the U.S. 2016 Presidential Election. It is not certain how Campaign events and Russian interference unfolded or possibly interacted. Wiki Leaks founder Julius Assange had a grudge against Hillary Clinton, and claims that she would have led the U.S. into war, spawning more terrorism. The Russians concluded that they had a better chance of influencing a President Trump than a President Clinton. John Podesta, former White House Chief of Staff for Bill Clinton, managed Hillary's 2016 Presidential Campaign. Someone hacked into Podesta's Campaign Computer, and delivered a treasure trove of embarrassing emails to Wiki Leaks. Thousands of Clinton Campaign emails appeared in the press. Clinton had to release thousands of emails sent and received on her home server during her tenure as Secretary of State.

Candidate Trump publically stated that he hoped the Russians would release thirty thousand of Hillary's missing emails if they had them. Trump actually encouraged Russian interference in the Campaign.

Trump's bromance with Putin likely does not depend on comradery or mutual respect between two authoritarian leaders. Golf writer James Dodson claimed that Donald Trump bragged about Russian money during play at Trump's National Golf Club in Charlotte. Dodson claimed in an interview with Boston's WBUR that Eric Trump, also at the match, confirmed availability of $100 million from Russian investors. Eric Trump denied the story. If Special Counsel Mueller can assemble a team of lawyers and forensic accountants to follow the Russian money, if any, as it traveled to and through the Trump Organization, the Russian Connection to Trump will be obvious. Russians may be holding mortgages on Trump Organization properties.

Trump has done his best to cover his tracks. He steadfastly refuses to release his tax returns, which would show his investments and creditors. Trump may be hoist by his own petard. By removing FBI Chief Comey, Trump brought about the appointment of Special Counsel Robert

Mueller, a former FBI Head. Mueller will have more independence than did Comey to conduct a thorough investigation, issue subpoenas, empanel a grand jury, and bring criminal charges if warranted by the evidence.

Trump uses intimidation as a tactic to gain advantage. In June 2017, a Trump friend announced that Trump was considering firing Special Counsel Mueller before he barely got started in his investigation. White House press aides quickly announced that the friend did not speak for the President. That way, Trump had the benefit of the intimidation, but not the burden. Special Counsel Mueller will carry on as if the threat never happened.

Mueller has wisely avoided engaging in a shouting match with Trump, who has taken pot shots at Mueller by sending out Tweets criticizing Special Counsel for friendship with former FBI Chief Comey and for employment of attorneys who contributed to Democrats, including Hillary Clinton.

Chapter 2

A Stormy Presidency, a White House in Chaos.

The White House is in chaos because of the disjointed, incoherent management style of President Trump, the firing of Comey, the appointment of a Special Counsel, the back channel to Moscow, and an unrelated compromise of intelligence. President Trump excluded U.S. media from a meeting on May 10, 2017, with the Russian Foreign Minister and Ambassador, and shared secret information with them that may jeopardize an Israeli spy at ISIS. The President may have committed Obstruction of Justice by asking FBI Director Comey to let go of the investigation of sacked Security Advisor Michael Flynn and possible collusion with the Russians by the Trump Campaign.

President Trump thought the solution to chaos would be to shake up the White House staff. As long as the president micromanages White House business haphazardly, disjointedly, and in a manner that suggests opposition to completion of the investigation into Russian interference, it will not help to appoint a new Press Secretary, Chief of Staff, or Director of Communications. Unitary Executive is necessary. It works, however, where the president delegates power to competent managers, and the president acts when fully briefed. When the president acts on whim, and cuts out his managers, policy becomes erratic.

From his numerous Campaign Statements, it looks as though Trump wanted to please the Russians. There are too many connections between the Trump Campaign and the Russians to call it a coincidence. Special Prosecutor Robert Mueller assembled a team of lawyers, accountants, and investigators to find the truth. In the meantime, Trump claims that no President has been treated so poorly. Trump's problem is that an ever-smaller circle outside his shrinking Base believes him. It appeared that Trump wanted to protect Lt. Gen. (Ret.) Michael Flynn from investigation to protect himself, or his son, Donald Trump, Jr., or his son in law, Jared Kushner. If so, Flynn may have headline making accusations to share with Special Counsel Mueller.

Whether by grant of immunity or reduction in charge, if Flynn violated the law, Muller will try to induce Flynn to cooperate. If the dots suggesting collusion with the Russians connect through Flynn's testimony, Impeachment is a possibility. Trump dismisses the Russia Investigation as a *'witch hunt'*.

Trump's most important job is managing and shaping public opinion. Whenever he feels the impulse, he coopts his press secretary and communications' staff. Trump is a master propagandist. He is expert at the *Big Lie* (*Grosse Lüge*), *Little Lie*, fibbing, smearing facts and fiction, and sowing confusion, doubts, resentment, ethnic, religious, and class tension, and suspicion. The Mueller investigation will assemble facts and resolve issues, including whether there is any evidence that the Trump Campaign colluded with Russia to disrupt or influence the U.S. 2016 Presidential Election.

It remains to be seen whether any Russians invested in the Trump Organization. Otherwise, Trump's blind spot toward Russia is difficult to explain. Special Counsel Mueller will need a bevy of forensic accountants to go over each Trump business and project for construction of a golf course, condominium, hotel, and office complex, to find out the source of invested capital. Mueller's *second biggest fight* will be to expose any collusion between the Russians and the Trump Organization and Campaign.

Mueller's biggest legal battle could be to force a sitting president to turn over his tax returns for the past five years, and to open for inspection the books, records, and financial statements of the Trump Organization. If the Supreme Court upholds Mueller's subpoenas, Donald Trump might make his last grand deal: resignation in exchange for immunity.

From the start, Donald Trump hampered his chance for success by allowing his ego salving needs to crowd out national presidential priorities. Though initially surprised at his win over Hillary Clinton, Trump immediately lost credibility by claiming a grand win. The White House spent weeks trying to spin Trump's win as a landslide. Trump fumed over photos that showed larger crowds for President Obama's 2009 Inauguration than for Trump's 2017 Inauguration. Trump lambasted his media staff for not making the world realize that Trump's election victory was the greatest. A visibly shaken Press Secretary, Sean Spicer, called a Saturday Press Conference to announce angrily that the Trump Inauguration was viewed by the largest number of people ever. Period.

The aerial photos, however, showed people viewing the Obama Inauguration where there were large sectors of snow-covered ground without spectators for Trump's Inauguration. Facts are stubborn things that do not go away. Spicer countered that Trump's television Inaugural audience was larger than Obama's. Trump spent five years on a propaganda campaign to show that President Obama was not born in the U.S. Trump knows that Republicans are unhinged in their fixation to obliterate all things Obama. Trump agrees with the GOP that the Affordable Care Act must repeal outright. Rational folks might consider amending the Act.

Trump snatched defeat from the jaws of victory by allowing his testy ego to reign supreme at the White House. The first order of business for the new President of the U.S. was to insult the President of Mexico and the Mexican People by insisting that Mexico would pay for an unnecessary wall along the southwest U. S. border to keep Mexican Nationals from emigrating illegally to the U.S. Trump launched his political campaign by appealing to America's prejudices. He set up Mexicans and Moslems as straw figures that he could strike down as the great Nationalist Crusader. The Border Wall and the Moslem Travel Ban were the centerpieces of his America First Campaign. He had to build the Wall because he promised his Base he would build a wall. Mexico had to pay for the Wall because he promised that, and there was no money in the U.S. Budget for a Border Wall.

Never mind that the net flow of Mexican Nationals across the U.S. Border since the 2008 Recession is in a southerly direction. According to Doris Meissner, Immigration Chief for President Clinton, Mexican immigration to the U.S. is at a twenty-five year low. Trump was twenty-five years too late with the Border Wall. Trump upbraided the President of Mexico in so many angry telephone calls that President Enrique Peña Nieto cancelled a planned visit to Washington. Except for the visit of British Prime Minister Teresa May, Trump's early days in the White House passed mostly on ego trips and jousting with windmills. Prime Minister May gave the Trump White House the template for conducting diplomatic events. Trump's flagging ego and testy demeanor, however, soon took back the reigns.

Trump engaged in a shouting match by telephone on 2/2/17 with Australia's Prime Minister, Malcolm Turnbull, over a prior promise by President Obama to take a number of refugees.

Trump overlooked the fact that Australia proved to be a strong ally of the U.S. in World Wars I and II, as well as in Korea, Viet Nam and beyond.

Trump's unquenchable need to win any competition shut out the Nation's Business, and took the gloss off Trump's win. He could not accept the fact that Hilary Clinton took nearly three million more popular votes than he did. He concluded that there had to be fraud for him to lose the popular vote. Trump announced *without any evidence* that three million or more undocumented immigrants in California and New York voted illegally for Hillary Clinton. Trump called for a Commission on Election Integrity to prove his claim, and rescue his wounded pride. Trump appointed Vice President Pence, Chair, and Kansas Secretary of State, Kris Kobach, Vice Chair.

In the meantime governors, legislatures, and secretaries of state in nearly thirty red states are moving forward with measures that effectively suppress progressive voters, including students, minorities, workers, and senior citizens. Trump's Commission will not find massive in person voter fraud, but may be a tool for vote suppression.

Kris Kobach's Data Mine.

Kris Kobach has a record of actions deemed as vote suppression. The American Civil Liberties Union successfully sued Kobach for unreasonably burdening citizens' right to vote. In response to an Order of the Tenth Circuit Court of Appeals, Kobach reinstated the disenfranchised voters to federal voter rolls but kept them off Kansas state voter rolls. ACLU attorneys applied for and received a follow up Court Order to restore the voters to state voter rolls.

Kobach's latest assault on liberty is a letter directed to the Secretaries of State of all fifty states requesting the names and addresses of all voters in each state, along with voting record, party affiliation, record of any felony conviction, and last four digits of Social Security Number. Kobach and Trump, of course, would try to use this information to purge progressive citizens from the voter rolls. To have this information in the hands of a Commission founded by Donald Trump and co-chaired by Chris Kobach is the beginning of a dictatorship. Most state Secretaries of State, including most Red States, have rejected the attempt by Trump and Kobach to data mine American democracy.

Attorney General Jeff Sessions brought a voter fraud case as U.S. Attorney in Shelby County, Alabama, in 1985. The NAACP successfully defended. Ronald Reagan nominated Sessions to be a judge of the U.S. District Court for the Southern District of Alabama. The Senate refused to confirm him based in part on opposition of civil rights groups.

Voter ID requirements are burdening minorities and seniors. Some African Americans, who have voted for fifty years, suddenly find they lack a state approved ID. In Red States, a hunting license may empower the holder to vote, but a student ID may not. States shutting down Department of Motor Vehicle Offices in predominately-black counties also hurts because DMV IDs and driver's licenses are usually the easiest identification to obtain. Republicans fear large voter turnout, but limiting citizens' right to vote automatically pits the GOP against African Americans, Hispanics and other minorities.

Trump Takes Control.

Sean Spicer had a difficult time at freewheeling press conferences during the first one hundred days. President Trump was furious. His Administration looked disorganized and unprepared. It was not Spicer's fault. Trump operated within a select group that included Jared Kushner and Vice President Mike Pence, based on input from Stephen Bannon and Stephen Miller. Spicer was not aware of what was going on. At press conferences, Spicer answered many inquiries by admitting that he had not discussed the topic with the President. Trump decided to take control. The object to control, for example, was not the Department of Defense. Trump delegated Defense to General Mattis.

The object was not the Justice Department. After Attorney General Jeff Sessions recused himself, Special Counsel Mueller took over the Russian Investigation as an independent prosecutor. The object was not the State Department, which angered Trump by not embracing his plan to lift sanctions on Russia. Trump took over what he considers the most important aspect of government by a minority elected president, the control of public opinion.

Molding public opinion sounds innocuous. At heart, however, shaping public opinion embraces propaganda and promotes the *Party Line*. Where necessary or convenient, the Leader can employ the *Big Lie*, the untruth that is so colossal that the public, or a substantial segment of the public, believes the *Big Lie* must be true. Otherwise, the Leader would not have put his reputation at risk by floating the *Big Lie* as gospel. Trump embraced the *Big Lie* as the foundation of his run for the presidency.

In 2011, Donald Trump became *Birther in Chief*. Trump started a five-year campaign to delegitimize President Obama by claiming that Obama was not born in the United States. At first blush, the birther strategy sounds like a minor fib that was more of a joke than a serious falsehood. By attacking President Obama's birth as foreign, however, Donald Trump galvanized the Republican Party behind him. Since Trump's political policy positions were not conservative, Trump had to prove his *bona fides* on social issues that appealed to conservatives. He embraced right to life and strict immigration. He added *Make America Great Again*, and *America First* for bringing back American jobs He appealed to Republicans and Reagan Democrats.

Candidate Donald Trump did not consider the attack on President Obama's American birth a minor matter. Trump publically reported *Confirming Lies* that he sent investigators to Hawaii to bring back documentary evidence that would prove President Obama was not born in Hawaii. Trump's investigators became missing persons, and never filed their report. A majority of Republicans, however, believed that President Obama is illegitimate.

They dismiss the classified notice of Barack Obama's birth in Honolulu on August 4, 1961, as part of a conspiracy by Obama's mother, who was planning long range to put her allegedly Kenyan-born son in the White House. Trump was not a conservative Republican. He might have run as a Democrat. The GOP was not impressed with Trump's bona fides. By floating the *Big Lie* as Birther in Chief, Trump made his bones with many Red States, if not with redstate.com.

Trump realizes that propaganda is too important to leave in the hands of Sean Spicer and Sara Huckabee Sanders. Trump understands that public opinion is the key to holding power in a Democracy. Trump is now acting as his own Minster of Propaganda. He has stripped Sean Spicer of all power. Press conferences frequently bar audio and video recording. Trump will personally handle release of information by sending Tweets and making statements himself. Trump molds public opinion through long-term strategic decisions. He understands that his worst enemy is the press and media, who will publish derogatory but truthful information about Trump and his Administration. To neutralize the power of the press and media, he is waging an ongoing attack on what he calls *"fake news"*.

During the Republican Primaries, Trump adopted tactics that fooled many naive observers, who thought Trump could not win by attacking Mexicans, Moslems, and Minorities. The guileless wondered if Trump knew what he was doing. Trump and his gurus, Stephen Bannon and Stephen Miller, knew exactly what they were doing. They were exploiting the frustration of the *White Working Class*, a natural constituency of Hillary Clinton and the Democrat Party. There is more to Democrats' corralling the labor vote, however, than gaining the endorsement of Union Leaders. Hillary had computers full of voter profiles of elites and the college-educated middle class. She lacked support of the base of the pyramid. Trump filled the vacuum created by the Democrats' abandonment of the White Working Class.

The Trump Bubble.

Having taken control of White House communications, Trump operates now in a media free bubble that insulates him from reality. Trump greeted the newly inaugurated President of South Korea, Friday, June 30, 2017. The cameras were on to capture the handshake. Trump immediately turned his back on the press and media reporters, and back patted the President of South Korea through the doors into the virtual world of the media free White House. Trump avoided responding to a reporter's question, *'Will you apologize to Mika Brzezinski'* [for saying that he would not allow her to join the Trump Party at Mira Lago because her face was allegedly bleeding from a face lift'].

Trump is conditioning reporters to stop criticizing Trump, or lose the protection of the First Amendment. Freedom of the Press is meaningless if the press cannot ask questions or make video or audio recordings. Trump has a long-term relationship with David Pecker, Chief Executive Officer of the *National Enquirer*. Joe Scarborough of MSNBC's *Morning Joe* alleged that Trump's White House Staff threatened him with an *Enquirer* smear if *Morning Joe* did not stop criticizing Trump. Joe refused to parrot the Party Line. The *Enquirer* published the article about Joe and Mika, but denied White House coordination.

Something is about to change fundamentally in the United States. The Nation will lose its democratic principles, or constitutional process will nip the Trump tyranny in the bud. It is no longer sufficient solace to the Nation for Melania to try to normalize belligerent or narcissistic behavior by claiming her husband is just fighting back in response to criticism from the media and the press. It is not helpful for Elaine Chao, Secretary of Transportation, to make excuses for Trump because he is new to the job. Trump has been gaming government (federal, state, and local) for fifty years. Because we have an unorthodox President, the Nation must cling to its democratic principles and constitutional process.

Former Speaker of the House Newt Gingrich must stop acting as a surrogate for this President when the President is engaged in petty squabbles or self-aggrandizement. Gingrich initially praised the appointment of Special Counsel Robert Mueller. Two weeks later, after the White House got to him, Gingrich raised questions about Mueller's impartiality as a friend of fired FBI Director James B. Comey. Speaker Paul Ryan, second in succession to the presidency, must call out Trump for any aberrant behavior and for dereliction of duty when the president is distracted from conducting the nation's business by self-absorbed ego salving diversions.

Watergate II?

It is extraordinary that there are so many investigations of the Trump Campaign and Presidency. The House and Senate Intelligence Committees, the FBI, and Special Counsel Robert Mueller are all investigating Russian interference in the U.S. 2016 Presidential election and possible collusion of the Trump Campaign with the Russians. Memorial Day weekend 5/28/17 saw new revelations of interest. Jared Kushner, Trump's son in law, business associate, and Senior Adviser, allegedly met with Russian Ambassador Kislyak during the campaign to set up a secret back channel of communications, using *Russian diplomatic facilities*, and *Russian communications equipment*.

General Michael Hayden (Ret.), former Head of NSA and CIA, excoriated the alleged back channel to Russia. *"What manner of ignorance, chaos, hubris, suspicion, contempt, would you have to have to think that doing this with the Russian Ambassador was a good or appropriate idea?"*

Paranoia.

Continuing with his analysis of the back channel on Saturday, 5/27/17 with Michael Smerconish on CNN, Haden pondered Trump's paralyzing fear of the Obama Administration. *"It says an awful lot about us as a society, that we could actually harbor those kinds of feelings that the organs of state would be used by my predecessor [President Obama] to come after me or to intercept my communications or to disrupt my administration in a way that made it seem legitimate to me to use the secure communication's facilities of a foreign power."…"It makes it even more odd that the foreign power in question was Russia."*

The actions of Trump and Kushner make sense in light of Russians' possible investment of money in the Trump organization. Kushner himself was in financial trouble partly because of his purchase of 666 Fifth Avenue, New York, on a two year 1.2 billion dollar note. Rents did not carry the monthly mortgage payment. When Ambassador Kislyak found out about Jared's financial problem, he reportedly advised Kushner to meet with Russian billionaire banker Sergey Gorkov and VEB Russia State Bank.

Blind Hatred/Fear of Obama.

Kushner was naive in discussing finance or a secret back channel with the Russians, using Russian facilities and Russian communications equipment. The flawed grown-ups in the room, Lt. Gen. (Ret.) Michael Flynn and President elect Donald Trump were so blind from hatred/fear of Obama, and by their own hubris, that neither of them could counsel Kushner to beware of the Russian trap. In fact, Flynn and Trump jumped enthusiastically into the Russian trap. Flynn had a personal score to settle. Obama agreed with pushing Flynn from his command for resisting civilian control at Defense Intelligence Agency in 2014.

Flynn previously acted as a top intelligence advisor on Iraq and Afghanistan to General Stanley McChrystal, who President Obama fired in 2010 after the general's criticisms appeared in a scathing article in the *Rolling Stone* panning U.S. defense policy and blowing off, as amateur meddling, suggestions offered by Vice President Biden for conducting the Afghan War.

Homeland Security Chief General (Ret.) John Kelly countered that it is normal and helpful to seek a back channel with those with whom the U.S. is not on the best of terms. Analyzing the alleged back channel to Russia, however, raises unanswerable suspicions. Kushner and Trump reportedly wanted to use Russian diplomatic facilities and equipment to communicate secrets to Russia. What targets did Kushner and Trump want to exclude by using a back channel to Russia? The excluded targets would not just include the New York Times, the Washington post, CNN, and the American People.

If Trump and Kushner used Russian facilities and Russian communications equipment, the excluded targets would include President Obama (until 1/20/17), the CIA, FBI, and Defense Intelligence Agency. Trump cannot have a private secret government to hide what he is doing from the American Government. The rumored back channel makes sense assuming Russian Oligarchs have invested hundreds of millions of dollars in the Trump Organization. The problem for Trump is that he favored the Russians from the start of his campaign. An interim Campaign Manager, Paul Manafort, represented Putin's man in Ukraine, Viktor Yanukovych. Carter Page, a Campaign Adviser, traveled frequently to Russia. General Michael Flynn took money from Russia and Turkey without Pentagon permission.

Trump appointed Secretary of State Rex Tillerson, former Exxon Mobile boss, whom President Putin awarded the Medal of Freedom for a contract to develop Russia's petroleum resources. Trump fired FBI Chief James B. Comey for pressing on with the investigation of the Russians, the Trump Campaign, and sacked National Security Adviser Michael Flynn. Trump publically urged, that if they had them, the Russians should release the thirty thousand missing emails of Hillary Clinton to Wiki Leaks for publication. In the context of all of the points of Russian contact with the Trump Campaign, the revelation is alarming that Jared Kushner allegedly negotiated a secret back channel to Russia. There are too many points of contact with Russia for Team Trump to dismiss them as harmless coincidences.

One action Trump can take to begin his rehabilitation as Chief Executive of the U.S., and not appear a Putin puppet, is to immediately expel Russian Ambassador Anatoly Antonov, who is the new Ambassador from Russia.

Special Counsel Mueller must determine the extent of Russian oligarchs' investments in the Trump Organization. If, as suspected, Russian oligarchs invested hundreds of millions of dollars in the Trump Organization, all of the points of contact with Russia make sense. If the Russian investments in the Trump Organization prove true, Trump and Jared Kushner doubtless approached the Presidency merely as an extension of doing business and making deals. The investigations likely will disclose conflicts of interest sufficient to start impeachment proceedings against Trump, based ultimately on dereliction of duty.

Trump's conflicts of interest are obvious for all to see from his conflicted conduct in the forced firing of National Security Adviser Michael Flynn, the gratuitous firing of FBI Chief Comey, and the recusal of Attorney General Jeff Sessions from representing the Justice Department in the Russian investigation. Team Trump is severely conflicted, and unable to discharge the duties of office. Investigations of the President hobble the U.S. Government.

Trump will resign the Presidency well before a newly elected House of Representatives adopts Articles of Impeachment in 2019, and likely, as soon as the Supreme Court upholds Mueller's subpoenas for Trump's tax returns, and the books, records, and financial statements of the Trump Organization. Donald Trump wants to do business deals and to develop real estate, office buildings, hotels, and golf courses. Trump does not want to govern a democratic Republic with two other independent, coequal branches of government in the legislature and judiciary tying his hands. Trump would relish the job of dictator, but that job is not possible in the U.S.

Trump will resign when he sees his hands tied by too many rules and regulations. Trump will resign when he sees that the Trump Organization cannot do deals because of the myriad investigations. Resignation will be complicated. Should Trump grant a pardon to Jared Kushner, just in case there could be a criminal investigation and prosecution by Special Counsel Mueller or the next Administration? Trump is on record saying that pardons prove guilt. Nevertheless, he cannot leave his son in law or his son, Don, Jr., in jeopardy.

Before resigning Trump will have to make a deal to protect Team Trump and the Trump Organization from prosecution, except if there is a serious espionage violation. Whoever flies high risks a fall, especially when treating the presidency as an opportunity to make commercial deals for private gain.

The Founders of our Nation knew what they were doing when they adopted a constitution with limited powers for the central government, with bright line demarcation and separation of powers among the Executive, Legislative, and Judicial Branches of Government, with checks and balances, and with an Emoluments Clause, which prohibits the Chief Executive from taking remuneration from foreign princes. There may not be a prohibition against the Executive having a business while in office. When the Executive, however, has such extensive business dealings as does the Trump Organization and Jared Kushner, the conflicts of business interests with the National interest prevent the President from properly executing the duties of office.

Jared Kushner's motives in negotiating a back channel to Russia may have been innocent, but is poisonous in the context of the Russian interference and intentional disruption of our democratic Republic.

The Russians played Team Trump for chumps. Trump and Kushner cannot sell their heritage for a bowl of porridge, or their country for investments of several hundred million dollars.

Wake up Team Trump. Expel Russian Ambassador Anatoly Antonov. The party is over for Putin. Trump does not need to shake up his staff. Trump needs to follow the lead of President Obama, who punished the Russians for interfering with the 2016 election. Obama closed the Russian recreation and espionage centers in New York and Maryland, and expelled 35 Russian diplomats and spies. Firing Sean Spicer will not rehabilitate Team Trump. Sending the Russian Ambassador to Siberia would be a good start to giving American back to the American People.

To rehabilitate themselves, Trump and Kushner must immediately pay back all Russian loans and investments, if any, in the Trump Organization and Kushner Company, and discontinue all commercial ties with Russia and Russian oligarchs. As an alternative, Trump can resign the Presidency. Trump has demonstrated over the past chaotic months that he cannot govern the United States because of conflicts arising from his ties to Russia.

Who recommended selection of Rex Tillerson as Secretary of State? Russia applauded Tillerson's selection. Tillerson is a loyal American, whom the Russians are using to their advantage. As former head of Exxon Mobil, Tillerson is in a commanding position to aid Russia in development of Russian petroleum reserves. Tillerson helped negotiate a multibillion-dollar contract with Russia for Exxon Mobil to bring American technology to Russian oil fields. President Putin awarded Tillerson the Medal of Friendship, formerly, Order of Lenin, for Tillerson's support of Russia. The Obama Administration stopped the Exxon Mobil contract with Russia by imposing sanctions on Russia for invading Crimea and eastern Ukraine in 2014.

The idea entertained by Trump, Tillerson, and Putin was that President Trump would lift sanctions against Russia, further denounce and ridicule former President Obama, and Exxon Mobil would bring American twenty first century technology to Russia's oil fields. Is there anyone in the United States who is surprised that President Putin wanted Donald Trump to win the U.S. 2016 presidential election? *Wake up President Trump! If not, Wake Up America!*

Trump Faults Obama for Not Acting Earlier On Russian Interference

President Trump tweeted the most bizarre statements on the weekend of June 23-26, 2017.He claimed that he just found out about Russian sabotage of the 2016 election. He noted that the CIA issued a report in October 2016 showing Russian interference. Trump asks tongue in cheek, *'Why didn't Obama do something about it earlier?'* CIA analysts may have briefed Trump in 2016 as a Presidential candidate on the Russian problem. Does he have a memory problem that he cannot remember the 2016 briefing in 2017? Or, is he rubbing President Obama's nose in Obama's inability to take decisive action against Russia before the 2016 election?

Obama, of course, feared the appearance of taking action to ensure the election of Hillary Clinton. President Obama should have released the Intelligence report in October, and at the same time, expelled Russian Ambassador Sergey Kislyak as well as the Russian diplomats and spies he expelled in January 2017.The new Russian Ambassador to the U.S. is Anatoly Antonov, a former Deputy Defense Minister. The European Union considers Antonov *persona non grata* over his role in covert Russian military subversion of eastern Ukraine.

Trump's twitterstorm went on to explain that in Trump's opinion, there was no Russian interference. What Trump did in 2016, however, fulfilled Vladimir Putin's wildest dreams. Trump claimed the election was rigged, and encouraged American public opinion to believe the election process corrupted, not by the Russians, but by the Democrats. Putin could not have had more success than with *The Manchurian Candidate.*

Trump's other disruptive tweet over that weekend confirmed that the Republican Healthcare Bill was *'mean'*. He wants the Healthcare Bill to have *'heart'*. GOP legislators, however, painted themselves into a corner by criticizing Obamacare as anathema for six years. Senator Rand Paul (R-KY) did not run for office to implement *'Obamacare Lite'*. The Obama Haters cannot function until they drive a stake through the heart of Obamacare. They cannot accept a revision of the Affordable Care Act of 2010 ("ACA"). Many Republicans, including Susan Collins (ME) and Dean Heller (NV) realize that their voters do not want a *'mean'* healthcare bill. GOP propaganda since 2010 turned public opinion against ACA. GOP poisoned the well from which they now must drink. Controlling two of three branches of government, the GOP can no longer blame Obama for all of the Nation's ills.

Chapter 3
A Cabinet of Generals, Billionaires & Two Women.

Except for the lapse in the appointment of Michael Flynn as National Security Adviser, President Trump excelled in choosing a solid Defense and Security Team. General Mattis, retired for four years, is a solid choice to head the Department of Defense, despite requiring a waiver for not showing separation from the military for at least seven years. General Marshall, for whom Congress enacted the waiver law in 1947, hoped that he would be the first and last military officer to require the waiver. It is a bedrock principle of American Government that the Nation's military should remain under civilian control.

General H.R. McMaster replaced Michael Flynn as National Security Adviser. Team Trump paraded McMaster out in May (looking a bit uncomfortable in civilian clothes) to assure the Nation that President Trump had not discussed *'resources'* or *'methods'* of intelligence gathering after the President revealed confidential intelligence about ISIS to Russia's Foreign Minister Sergey Lavrov and Ambassador Sergey Kislyak.

In a gesture of counterintuitive hyperbole, McMaster offered that, *"It was entirely appropriate for the President"* to disclose highly classified intelligence to the Russians. Presidents have the unique power under U.S. law to declassify secrets on the spot. Presidents have immunity from prosecution in security matters that lesser government officials lack. McMaster, however, did not address the concern of the intelligence community that the Russians and ISIS could reverse engineer the information supplied by Trump to make reasonable conclusions about sources and methods utilized to gather the highly sensitive information, namely, the order of battle for ISIS in Syria. Israel, which supplied the information, emphasized that its relation with the U.S. was solid (thereby hoping that President Trump would be more tractable and generous than was President Obama in the opinion of Prime Minister Netanyahu).

General John Kelly provides welcome steadiness at Homeland Security. Kelly will have to keep an eye on the Constitution and the laws as the President tries to enforce his Moslem Ban.

President Trump did appoint women to his cabinet. He chose Betsey De Vos as Secretary of Education. De Vos was a billionaire in her own right. She married another billionaire. Public school supporters criticized the nomination of De Vos, who has no experience (personal or professional) with America's Public School System. She is a firm believer in vouchers and privatization of select schools. Her thinking on education matters is mainstream Republican, similar to policies espoused by former Florida Governor and presidential contender Jeb Bush. The problem with vouchers and privatization of select schools is that those programs cannibalize money, resources, and personnel from public schools.

The urban areas of the U.S. house the largest concentration of minorities in the Nation. Social conservatives migrated in the 1960s through 1980s and beyond to the suburbs to get away from living near minorities. As the same time, those same social conservatives migrated by the tens of millions from the Democratic Party to the Republican Party.

Nearly one hundred years after the Civil War Amendments to the Constitution, Congress enacted legislation that would bring political equality to former slaves. The right to vote is the spring from which all other political rights flow. The era of Jim Crow would soon be a relic of a shameful past.

Because of these neighborhood and party migrations, the Republicans in general are not enthusiastic about appropriating money to acquire resources or personnel for public schools in urban areas. No Republican votes, no money. Vouchers and privatization exacerbate the already desperate condition of urban public schools. Consider what happens to a Flint, MI, for example, if vouchers are available for families to remove their children to private schools. A strained public school system sustains additional strain until it becomes dysfunctional. The families and students who flee the public school system with voucher funding generally are somewhat more upscale and capable than are the families and students left behind.

The achievement of the students left behind tends to diminish. The budget of the public school system reduces by the amount of money diverted. The downward spiral of the urban public school system intensifies.

The Senate confirmed Rex Tillerson Secretary of State on 1 Feb 2017. Tillerson came as a last minute choice, after the President considered political choices such as Rudy Giuliani, Chris Christie, and former Speaker Newt Gingrich. Tillerson was part of the Russia strategy. Team Trump would remove sanctions against Russia to allow the Exon-Mobil contract with Russia's

Rosneft Oil Company to go forward. Tillerson was in a unique position as former CEO of Exxon Mobil and a person President Putin knew and respected.

The Senate confirmed Jeff Sessions Attorney General on 8 Feb 2017. As the first Senator to support candidate Trump, Sessions had a great deal of influence on Trump. Stephen Miller, Trump's senior adviser on policy, was Communications Director for Senator Sessions. Miller writes Nationalist speeches for Trump, and worked on the Moslem Travel Ban with Stephen Bannon.

The problem with some of Trump's Cabinet is that they head departments or agencies that Republicans want to dismantle. Environmental Protection Agency is at the top of the hit list. Scott Pruitt's job at EPA is not to protect the environment. Pruitt's job is to make life easier for industrialists like Charles and David Coke of Coke Industries. The Coke Brothers spend millions to support GOP candidates and to lobby against regulations that burden industry. When Wisconsin voters held a recall election against Governor Scott Walker, the Coke Brothers spent ten million dollars and sent a propaganda Bus to each county to educate the voters. Scott Walker prevailed.

Republicans have advocated doing away with Department of Education for years. Every Senate session, GOP introduces a bill to eliminate Department of Education. There is a bill pending now. EPA is also in danger.

Chapter 4

Twitter Storm—What President Trump's Tweets Mean.

Donald John Trump entered the world as the son of a privileged family. His father Fred Trump was a real estate developer. The family lived in Queens, New York. The father built low-income apartments in Queens and Brooklyn. As a boy, Donald had just about everything a boy could want. There was always tension, however, between father and son. The father naturally was more serious. Donald just wanted to have fun. Donald did not always listen to his father's instructions. Or, Donald listened and found ways to get around his father's rules. Donald was quite comfortable at home. Fred Trump became more frustrated with Donald's rebellious behavior. Donald traveled to Manhattan a few times without permission.

Fred decided that Donald needed more structure in his life. Fred sent Donald to military boarding school. Since sent away at thirteen, Donald never trusted authority of any person or thing that could tell him what to do. Donald wanted to be the boss to escape authority of others.

Donald's grandfather Friedrich Drumpf emigrated to the U.S. from Kallstadt in Germany's Rheinland Palatinate district. Friedrich changed his name to Frederick Trump when he took U.S. citizenship, thereby making it possible for Donald Trump to run for President one hundred thirty years later. *Some voters in the U.S. would not take Donald Drumpf seriously as a presidential candidate.* It is ironic that the grandson of an immigrant would make his mark in politics by attacking Mexicans, Moslems, and undocumented immigrants in general. *All of Trump's grandparents and his mother were foreign born.*

Trump's mother came from Scotland to work in the U.S. as a domestic, and later married Trump's father, Fred. Trump's grandfather Fred (Friedrich) made money in restaurants, and set up a company in his wife's name. This company ultimately became Trump Organization. While working for his father in their construction business, Trump paled around with the workers in Queens and Brooklyn. That allows the billionaire to imagine he represents the working class.

That did not stop Trump the wheeler-dealer from putting his casinos into bankruptcy four times or from welching on various contracts so he could force his contractors and suppliers to accept a reduction in contract price. After trying extraordinary measures to avoid liability, President Trump finally settled the class action lawsuit against Trump University by paying Twenty Five Million Dollars. Among Trump's strategies to stifle the Trump University claim was to blame U.S. District Court Judge Gonzalo Curiel of prejudice. Trump's logic was linear but absurd. The judge's parents are Mexican, although the judge was born in Indiana. Trump campaigned on building a wall on the U.S. southwest border. Therefore, the judge is prejudiced against Trump. QED.

Trump and his guru Stephen Bannon, former Executive of Breitbart News, devised a strategy to win the Electoral College vote, whether losing the popular vote or not, by appealing to the basest instincts of the bottom of the base of the electorate. The little people were pissed, and it showed.

Trump's rallies drew large enthusiastic audiences of angry workers, while Hillary was taking six hundred thousand dollars from Goldman Sachs for a speech. Trump was an unusual candidate in that he communicated late at night and in the early morning by sending out tweets. These tweets are a roadmap, often distorted, to what is on Trump's mind. His tweets cannot be taken at face value, however. Someone or something might be bothering Trump. He might tweet an insult or a lie to try to even the playing field. Trump attacked the press and the media almost daily because he knows that truthful reporting will frequently make Trump look bad. The first thing every tin horn dictator does is to attack journalists in an effort to suppress criticism.

Trump's billionaire Commerce Secretary Wilbur Ross was impressed that there were no protests during the Trump entourage's visit to Saudi Arabia in May 2017. *"Not one guy with a bad placard."* Ross was blissfully unaware that dissent can be a capital offense in Saudi Arabia, if the King feels threatened.

Trump uses Twitter and sends Tweets to intimidate, to punish, to spread propaganda, and to keep his Base fired up. He uses Tweets to send up trial balloons like his naive suggestion to form an impenetrable cyber security unit with Putin to keep elections safe. Trump is his own worst enemy because he detracts from statesmanlike issues and pronouncements by mingling important matters with barroom brawls with talk show hosts. He attacks the press and the media as *'fake news'* because he knows the truth will often make him look bad. He attacks his own intelligence agencies because they are investigating Russian interference in the 2015-2016 election, and possible collusion of the Trump Campaign.

He controls White House release of news by banning audio or video recording, or both. He cannot control the facts, however. Top Campaign Aides—including Jeff Sessions, Jared Kushner, and Lt. Gen. (Ret) Mike Flynn—failed to disclose meetings with Russians on their Security Questionnaires. Paul Manafort and Donald Trump, Jr. kept quiet about their meeting with Natalia Veselnitskaya 6/9/16. Manafort and Flynn registered after the fact as Foreign Agents.

Retaliatory Tweets.

Trump fights back critics with tweets. Islamic terrorists attacked in London on June 3, 2017, killing twelve. The Mayor of London Sadiq Khan denounced the barbaric attack, and informed the people that there would be in increased presence of armed police in the streets of London. The Mayor urged people not to be alarmed, referring to presence of armed police. Donald Trump tweeted that Islamic terrorists killed people, and the Mayor said not to be alarmed. Why did the President of the United States intentionally take the Mayor of London's remarks out of context? Trump's tweet was not a mistake or a misunderstanding. Trump was settling a score with the Mayor, who had criticized Trump in 2016 for the proposed Moslem Travel Ban. The U.S. Ambassador to the U.K. promptly issued a statement in support of the Mayor of London.

Trump Attacked His Own Justice Department.

On 6/4/17 Trump fumed that the Justice Department should have appealed the original Moslem Ban—not the watered down version—apparently unaware that both texts of the ban were promulgated pursuant to separate Executive Orders signed by Trump as President. The "watered down" version of the Moslem ban came with the last signed Executive Order, and generally would be controlling. Trump does not like the government because it taxed and regulated Trump as a businessperson.

Trump does not like the Justice Department because Acting Attorney General Sally Yates informed White House Counsel Don McGahn in January 2017 that the Russians could blackmail National Security Adviser Lt. Gen. (Ret.) Michael Flynn because Flynn lied about discussing sanctions with Russian Ambassador Sergey Kislyak. Trump felt pressured, and fired Flynn twenty-four days later.

State Department angered Trump by not enforcing his Moslem travel ban and by not lifting the Russian sanctions imposed by President Obama. Obama's sanctions frustrated Trump's grand plan to start the transfer of American oil drilling technology to Russia through the Exxon Mobil contract with Rosneft. Trump retaliated by cutting State's budget by twenty-five percent. Sally Yates announced she would instruct U.S. Attorneys not to support the Moslem Travel Ban. Trump fired Yates three hours later.

Trump is furious that Attorney General Jeff Sessions recused himself from the investigation into Russian interference into the 2016 presidential election. Trump assumed he could control the Russian investigation through Sessions. Trump fired FBI Chief Comey to allow Trump to gain more control over the probe. With Sessions out of the loop through self-recusal, Rod Rosenstein, Deputy Attorney General takes Sessions place in deciding matters related to the Russian investigation. Rosenstein, a stickler for maintaining integrity and public confidence, appointed Robert Mueller, former FBI Chief, to head the Russian investigation.

Trump is now worse off than before he fired Comey. As independent counsel. Mueller can empanel a grand jury and seek indictments. If Trump fires Mueller, there will be cries of *Saturday Night Massacre*—reprising the firestorm that erupted after President Nixon fired Archibald Cox as Watergate Special Prosecutor.

Trump Exhausts Controversy.

Casual observers do not understand Donald Trump's secret to dealing with controversy. He has no shame, and never admits he is wrong. He is a master propagandist and a master manipulator of public opinion. His target group for political purposes is the base of the pyramid, with a bias toward the White Working Class. He is not concerned about the opinion held of him by elites, college professors, progressives, pundits, reporters, the media, or the press. He can and does create his own virtual reality. He is a master of the *Big Lie* (*Grosse Lüge*). As perfected by der Führer, he instinctively takes aim at marginal groups, to the delight of more dominant groups. He plans his moves. He might have run as a Democrat in an earlier election cycle. He decided, however, to run in 2016 as a Republican.

He made his move against President Obama in 2011 by claiming the President was not born in the Unites States. He continued the *Big Lie* as drum major for the Birther Movement until 2016, when he unapologetically walked away from the *Big Lie* about President Obama's birth.

Most public figures would shy away from controversy. Many would cut their losses early to ease the pain. Trump will endure a lot of pain to get his way. His Base of 34% of the public thinks more of him for standing up to the media, the press, and the Government.

Trump Looks As Though He Is Hiding Something.

Why is the President of the United States jumping through hoops backwards to try stop the investigation into Russian interference in the 2016 presidential election? If he has nothing to hide, why is he against the investigation into Russian interference in the 2016 election?

Trump At War With the World.

Having his way all the time for so long has made Trump unable to accept the daily disappointments, reverses, challenges, and criticisms that ordinary folks endure. Trump purchased Atlantic City casinos at grossly inflated prices. One analyst reported that that the casinos would have to handle a million dollars a day, which he doubted, or fail. Trump had the analyst fired from one publication. Trump's father, Fred, purchased one million dollars in casino chips that he never cashed in to try to bailout his son. Trump filed bankruptcy for the casino companies multiple times, overturning leases, contracts, and labor agreements.

He used litigation to vanquish his opponents. If someone sued, he would look for a way to countersue to gain advantage over those who could not afford the attorneys' fees needed for ongoing pleadings, motions, and trial, followed by an appeal. Trump frequently refused to pay contractors, telling them to settle for one-half or two-thirds of the agreed price. Take it or leave it, was his attitude.

He became a dictator on his television show, *'The Apprentice'*. He controlled the script and the players. On a whim, or for spite, he would simply say, *'You're fired'*, and the person would disappear from the show. He had his way with women. He bragged about his exploits on the infamous tape on the *Access Hollywood* Bus Ride with Billy Bush. He explained how he would just start kissing beautiful women. He could do anything he wanted to women because he was famous. He could grope women at will. The tape became public on October 7, 2016. The release helped Trump because it coincided with a statement by President Obama concerning Russian interference in the 2016 election. NBC news fired Billy Bush from *Access Hollywood, apparently for not condemning Trump on the tape*. Trump survived the notoriety, and went on to win the Electoral College Vote.

Secret Trump Government.

After election, the Trump Transition Team, headed by Jared Kushner, tried to set up a back channel to Russia, using Russian diplomatic facilities and Russian communications equipment. Team Trump considered Russia the good guy, possibly because of multi-million dollar investment in the Trump Organization by Russian billionaires. Team Trump mistrusted the U.S. Government. Trump would keep the back channel a secret from the CIA, FBI, and Defense Intelligence Agency. In short, Trump would operate a secret government alongside the U.S. government. Russian Ambassador Sergey Kislyak referred Jared Kushner to Sergey Gorkov and VEB Bank, perhaps to help Kushner to refinance the $1.2 billion mortgage note against his company's building at 666 Fifth Avenue.

Kushner reportedly discussed the secret back channel with Gorkov .Russia owns VEB Bank. By law, the Chairman must be the Russian Prime Minister. Gorkov is a graduate of the spy school college operated by the FSB (State Security Service) successor to the KGB. The Russians played Team Trump for fools. Putin could not have asked for more than Team Trump to help Putin to tear apart Western Democracies.

Trump's tweets mean that he is nervous, fearful, or outraged about something. First, it was Hilary Clinton's win of the popular vote by nearly three million. Next, it was the FBI investigation by Director James B. Comey. Trump fired Comey, and felt relieved of pressure. Trump's firing of Comey triggered appointment of Special Counsel Robert Mueller to head an investigation independent of Justice Department control. Reports surfaced that Mueller scheduled interviews with Dan Coats, Director of National Intelligence, and Admiral Mike Rogers, Head of NSA, to probe whether President Trump tried to enlist them to ask Comey to back off the investigation into Russian interference in the 2016 election and possible collusion of the Trump Campaign with the Russians.

Trump responded with the Mother of All Tweets. *'You are witnessing the single greatest WITCH HUNT in American history—led by some very bad and conflicted people'*, 6/15/17.Trump is worried that some of Muller's hires for the Russian Investigation contributed to the Democratic Party. Trump is following in the footsteps of the only president in U.S. history who resigned to avoid impeachment. President Nixon asked CIA Director Richard Helms to inform the FBI Director that the disclosure of the source of the Watergate hush money would jeopardize national security. Nixon confused his holding on to power with ensuring the safety of the Nation. Nixon failed to corrupt the CIA and the FBI. The Senate Intelligence Committee called DNI Director Coats and NSA Director Rogers to testify. Both invoked Executive Privilege, and refused to confirm or deny that President Trump asked them to request FBI Director Comey to back off the Russian Investigation.

On 6/16/17 Trump tweeted, *'I am being investigated for firing the FBI Director by the man who told me to fire the FBI Director! Witch Hunt'*. We are witnessing a Kabuki Dance at the highest level of Government. Trump fretted over the FBI Investigation into Russian interference in the U.S. 2016 Presidential election. Trump reached out to FBI Director James B, Comey on several occasions to try to enlist Comey as a Trump cheerleader, who would back off the investigation of the Russians and Trump's sacked National Security Adviser, Lt. Gen. (Ret.) Michael Flynn. Comey sent body language messages to Trump on numerous occasions to let Trump know that he would not back off the FBI investigations. Trump decided that he would fire Comey to ease the pressure he felt from the FBI investigations. Trump called in Attorney General Sessions and Deputy Attorney General Rod Rosenstein, and asked them for advice on firing Comey.

Rosenstein wrote a memorandum that criticized Comey for, among other things, usurping the prerogative of the Justice Department by the FBI Director's announcement that there would be no prosecution of Hillary Clinton for email irregularities during her tenure as Secretary of State. Attorney General Sessions agreed with Rosenstein's memo, and fired Comey. Rosenstein, acting independently to preserve the integrity of the Department of Justice, appointed former FBI Director Robert Mueller Special Counsel to head up an independent investigation of Russian interference in the 2016 election. In view of Trump's attempts to get Comey to back off, followed by Trump's abrupt dismissal of Comey, Special Counsel Mueller likely will also investigate Trump for Obstruction of Justice.

Former House Speaker Newt Gingrich declared that a president could not be guilty of Obstruction of Justice. This is an interesting concept, possibly flowing from the idea of the president as the unitary executive and chief law enforcer, subject only to impeachment and removal from office by the Congress as provided in the Constitution. Gingrich ignores the fact that the House may include Obstruction of Justice as an Article of Impeachment. In a sense, Gingrich is correct. The Justice Department or a Special Counsel acting as a Prosecutor likely would submit a report of facts to the Congress rather than file a Criminal Complaint against the president for Obstruction of Justice.

This is what happened in the case of President Richard Nixon, who clearly supervised the cover-up of the Watergate Burglary. As the Chief Executive, the President can dismiss or order dismissal of any Justice Department attorneys and other employees including the Attorney General and Special Prosecutor.

Chapter 5

President Trump Forced To Pivot Toward Reality

It has taken nearly eighteen months, but President Trump is starting to make a small pivot away from the iconoclastic, xenophobic, nationalistic rabble-rouser that he portrayed during the primary, through the general election, and into the first hundred or so days in the White House. Trump's hardcore fans, perhaps a third of the Electorate, loved the insulting invective and unpredictable spontaneity of their idol, who was untethered to any coherent political belief or rational plan for governance. Trump concluded that he owed his election to his Base. He would not abandon them after the Inauguration. The mutual loyalty between Trump and his fans set up a metaphysical paradox. For more than a year, Trump had been making reckless statements and unrealistic promises that he could not fulfill. The chaos of the first hundred days in office demonstrated in real time that he could not continue on the path set during the Campaign.

Aside from the nomination of Court of Appeals Judge Neil Gorsuch to the Supreme Court, and appointment of a solid national security team, Trump accomplished little in the first hundred days, or first six months. Democrats could not support the nomination of Judge Gorsuch after Senate Majority Leader Mitch McConnell (R-KY) refused to hold hearings to consider the merits of Judge Merrick Garland, whom President Obama nominated in March 16, 2016 after the passing of Justice Antonin Scalia. As the hundred day in office mark approached, Team Trump panicked and called for immediate Repeal and Replacement of Obamacare.

Nearly seven years after passage of Obamacare, Republicans never had a serious alternative healthcare plan. They only knew that because Obama embraced the *Affordable Care Act* ('ACA'), they hated it. The House of Representatives developed a special skill set for repealing ACA, spewing out about five dozen mostly redundant ACA Repeals from 2011-2017.

It was a rite of passage for newly sworn GOP House Members from 2010-2017 to file their very own ACA Repeal Bill. It was how they made their bones, and impressed GOP House Leadership with their bona fides. The Senate, of course, studiously ignored the six-year blizzard of House ACA floggings.

Trump bragged that he canceled the Trans Pacific Partnership ("TPP") trade agreement. The U.S. however, *never* adopted the TPP. Trump boasted that he would terminate the North American Free Trade Agreement ("NAFTA"). Republican Governors in farm states explained to Trump that the U.S. benefited by exporting millions of dollars of agricultural products through NAFTA. Trump will not cancel NAFTA. Trump threatened to withdraw from the Paris Climate Accord, and did so on June 1, 2017, agreeing with the Republican fiction that the weather and climate are independent of human industrial activity. The Europeans are aghast that Trump ignores climate problems and the link to industrial pollution. Trump will be unable to fulfill his promise to bring back the jobs that left America in the past fifty years.

In short, Trump's unrealistic, nationalist, xenophobic agenda is a Potemkin City of cardboard fantasy. That is why repeal of ACA was the sole possible legislative accomplishment for Trump's first hundred days or first six months. House Speaker Paul Ryan thought he could square the circle, that he could repeal ACA, replace it with a bill that would appear to provide affordable healthcare, and not add to the deficit.

House Leadership called for a vote on repeal and replace ACA within the Trump one hundred day metric as a sop to Trump's embarrassingly short list of accomplishments. Ryan christened the Bill with a patriotic title, *The American Health Care Act*, to contrast with ACA, which Republicans shunned as *'other'* because President Obama touched it. The GOP Bill failed to pass because a number of Republicans feared voter retribution over the stripped down healthcare measure. After seven years of benefiting from ACA, more Americans supported ACA than opposed it. Faced with failure, Trump denounced the one hundred day standard as meaningless. A week later, the House passed a slightly improved, but still unacceptable ACA Repeal and Replace Bill.

The Senate will pass its own healthcare bill. A Conference will use the Senate's improved provisions to shore up the bare bones House Bill, which the Congressional Budget Office forecast would leave twenty three million Americans without healthcare.

Trump praised the House Healthcare Bill sponsored by Speaker Ryan at a Rose Garden commemoration, until the Senate declared the bare bones bill dead on arrival. Trump has no core policies, and little understanding of the issues. Trump is a weathervane that frequently points in the direction suggested by the last person he speaks to. He repositioned and declared the House Bill *"mean"*. He hoped the Senate Healthcare Bill would be more generous. The Senate, however, drafted their bill in secret, and without hearings or participation by stakeholders, the media, or the public. Senator Bob Corker cautioned that, *'The process is better if you do it in public'*. Trying to gloss over the secrecy of the GOP process, Senate Majority Leader McConnell declared deceptively, *'Look we've been dealing with this issue for seven years. It's not a new thing.'*

The problem, however, is that the GOP *ignored* healthcare for seven years. The GOP should have developed a healthcare bill in 2010. The GOP turned its back on the ACA only because President Obama embraced it.

The 2017 Senate Healthcare Bill presents the worst of both worlds. Progressives opposed the Bill because the Senate cut back Medicaid and gave tax benefits to the wealthy. Conservatives object because the Bill does not cut deep enough. Rand Paul (KY), Ted Cruz (TX), Mike Lee (UT) and Ron Johnson (WS) oppose because the Bill appears to be a revision to the ACA. They want to drive a stake through the heart of Obamacare, and repeal it outright. Senate Majority Leader Mitch McConnell (KY) is taking heat for hiding the bill from the pubic until just before the vote. Senate Security removed Dozens of protesters physically removed from McConnell's office area. President Obama labelled the Bill the largest transfer of tax benefits in history from the middle class and poor to the wealthy.

McConnell can only afford to lose two Republican Senators' votes if the Democrats solidly oppose. Lisa Murkowski AK), Susan Collins (ME), Rob Portman (IN), and Dean Heller (NV) think the bill cuts too much from the middle class.

During the Campaign, Trump promised that, if elected, he would build a wall along the southwest border, and that Mexico would pay for it. Trump likely was playing the crowd with something he knew was not going to happen. He never promised to build a wall, *for which the U.S. would pay*. The promise of a wall always depended on Mexico paying the bill. Trump must have known that no Mexican president could grovel to the U.S. and agree to fund a wall to keep Mexicans from crossing into the U.S. without a visa. Trump and his advisers had to know that there was no money in the Ryan Budget to build a wall. His Base could not blame him for not building a wall. The blame would fall on Mexico and Speaker Ryan.

The promise of building a wall with Mexico's money soon became a distant memory of meaningless Campaign puffery and buffoonery.

Trump attacked the Obama legacy as if his political life depended on it. Trump signed a dozen or more Executive Orders to try to eliminate all traces of Obama's hand in federal rules governing coal mining, education, energy, environmental protection, healthcare, and justice. Trump emulated the Egyptian Pharaohs, some of whom chiseled away the name of their predecessor from granite memorials. Trump, however, is stuck with Obama comparisons and standards set. Whatever healthcare bill emerges as law will contain many of the popular provisions of Obamacare, despite the new patriotic sounding name of the House skeletal Bill. In preparing the first speech of Melania Trump as First Lady Elect, Team Trump copied ideas and text from a speech given by Michelle Obama.

When Melania Trump deplaned with the President in Saudi Arabia on the first Trump trip abroad, she copied Michelle Obama and did not wear a headscarf to placate Moslem sensibilities. When Michelle Obama appeared in Riyadh without the headscarf, Trump publically criticized her. Laura Bush shunned the headscarf as well. When the first couple visited the Pope, Melania wore a head veil as a tribute to her Catholic faith. At all events, the Pope reportedly requires women to wear a head covering. The Saudi King does not. Trump notably banned Sean Spicer, the only Catholic serving in Trump's inner circle, from attending the audience with the Pope. Trump, the master propagandist and master publicist, sees Spicer as a dispensable amateur.

During the Campaign, Trump declared that Islam hates us. He and the GOP criticized President Obama for not condemning Radical Islamic Terrorism by name. Republicans insisted that it is impossible for the U.S. to defeat an enemy before defining it and naming it. President Obama did not want to wage war against Islam. On his trip to Saudi Arabia, Trump emulated his nemesis and made no mention of Radical Islamic Terrorism. Trump urged the Saudis and dozens of Conferees from nearly every Moslem Nation to drive terrorists out, without denoting them as Islamic. *In fact, Trump is slowly making the long awaited pivot, however late and however disjointed and incoherent.* Conventional wisdom expected the pivot after the GOP primary campaign concluded in Trump's nomination. Candidates of both parties run primaries to the edge where their base resides, and move to the center during the general election campaign.

Most of the pundits thought Trump could not win if he refused to pivot. As Trump maintained the primary strategy into the general election campaign, the media saw no path to 270. The media reported the opinion—of *'no path'* to victory for Trump—as a virtual fact. The fiction of the *Blue Wall* was that the Trump Campaign would crash on the Democratic strongholds of Wisconsin, Michigan, and Pennsylvania. Trump's primary strategy prevailed, and he won the 2016 election without making a pivot. After nearly six months of chaos in the White House, however, Trump proved to himself that the world is not ready for President Rambo. There is nothing like on the job training to temper strained principles and impractical goals. U.K. Prime Minister Teresa May showed Trump early on how to conduct an effective reception of a visit by Head of a Foreign Government.

Trump had to realize that the U.K. visit was a positive result. He had to know that—the shouting match he had by telephone with Australia's President, and the weeks of pressure with Mexican President Peña Nieto over an unnecessary and spiteful wall—were failures.

Trump's Base would be pleased if Trump scolded Moslems to their face in Riyadh for not rooting out Radical Islamic Terrorists by name. After four months in office, Trump is beginning to realize that he is the duly elected President of all Americans and that there is a diplomatic and strategic objective to the exercise of Executive Power. If Trump performs well for the remainder of his term, he could win reelection without his Base. He needs the Saudis on his side now, more than he needs his Base. He already repaired relations with Australia.

He can mend fences with Mexico unless he wants to keep Mexico as a Piñata to hit figuratively with a stick whenever his Base needs stimulation. Trump is slowly realizing that the scorched earth policies and conspiracy theories of Breitbart News and Info Wars are not helpful to the conduct of Government business or international affairs.

Virtual Reality Meets Ms. Reality

What the Nation is seeing in real time is the playing out of a Greek Tragedy. Trump as would be autocrat took over a government riddled with progressives who believe in one-person one vote, in the democratic election process, and in the rule of law. His election had fatal flaws because of Russian interference. To uphold the foundation of the electoral process, the Nation must probe the extent of Russian interference and any possible collusion of Team Trump with the Russians. Trump must stifle the investigation because the result could stamp his election illegitimate. It is poetic and ironic justice that Trump, *Birther in Chief*, should face the brand of illegitimacy on his presidency. In 2011, Trump started his own campaign to delegitimize his predecessor by alleging, without any evidence, that President Obama was not born in the United States, and, therefore, not qualified under the Constitution to serve as president.

To protect his legacy and his incumbency, Trump must quash the investigation into Russian interference with the 2016 election. As Chief Executive of the United States, Donald John Trump has the power to frustrate and defeat any investigation undertaken by the *ordinary* organs of the *Executive* Branch. He cannot stop an investigation by the Congress. The investigation by the Executive Branch is now in the hands of Special Counsel Robert Mueller, former head of the FBI. As Chief Executive, President Trump has the power to fire Mueller. He likely would face Impeachment for doing so. Presidents who fire a Special Counsel, who is investigating the president, do so at their peril. Richard Nixon learned this lesson after firing Archibald Cox, Special Prosecutor to the Watergate Investigation.

Trump's Attraction to Russia.

Trump's fascination with Russia stems from his financial problems in the U.S. Trump led his companies into bankruptcy four times from 1991 to 1994. New York banks refused to lend to Trump because of his cavalier attitude toward the obligation to pay off promissory notes. Deutsche Bank lent Trump money in 2014 to renovate the old post office building in Washington as a hotel. Trump owes about $300 million to Deutsche Bank, which, in and of itself, presents a sizeable conflict of interest. Federal regulators are seeking up to $14 billion from Deutsche Bank to settle claims that the bank allegedly issued toxic mortgages that failed in the housing crisis starting in 2008.

Blackballed by most banks in New York, Trump became fascinated with Russia. Government regulations were fewer in Russia than in the U.S. The number of entrepreneurs, millionaires, and billionaires had grown dramatically under Putin. If a businessperson could stay in the good graces of Putin, the Russian oligarchs had billions to invest. Trump took the Miss Universe Pageant to Russia in 2013. He made friends with Aras Agaralov, an oligarch, and his son Emin, a pop music star. Rob Goldstone, Emin's music publicist, later wrote emails to Donald Trump, Jr, asking if Team trump could meet with Natalia Veselnitskaya, a Russian attorney

In a later email, Goldstone suggested that Russia supported Trump's candidacy and that the attorney had information from the state prosecutor's office that would incriminate Hillary Clinton. Donald, Jr., showed remarkable transparency. *"If it is what you say, I love it."*

Trump, Sr. was impressed by Russian money, and not worried about falling out of favor with Putin. Falling out of favor with Putin, however, was a risk experienced by Bill Browder, CEO of Hermitage Capital Management. Browder took Hermitage to Russia in 1996 with seed capital of $25 million. He made a strategic mistake of investing in Gazprom, and other Russian *State-Owned* Companies. As a shareholder, he complained of corruption and diversion of assets by insiders close to the Kremlin.

In 2006, the Russian Government classified Browder as a "threat to national security." The insiders saw their livelihoods at risk because of Browder's insistence on adherence to generally accepted accounting principles and preservation of corporate assets, whether the corporation was state-owned or private. Gangsters physically assaulted Browder, his attorneys, accountants, associates, and relatives. In a Kafkaesque sting, gangsters raided Hermitage offices, stole corporate documents, and defrauded the Russian Government of a tax refund of $230 million.

Sergei Magnitsky, an independent auditor, disclosed details of the fraud perpetrated by gangsters. Putin arrested Magnitsky, and charged him with the crime Magnitsky discovered. Prosecutors pressured Magnitsky to confess to the crime committed by mobsters. Magnitsky refused, and died in a Russian jail on 1/16/09 at age 37.

Browder fled for his life from Russia, and lobbied for sanctions against Putin and certain mobsters. The U.S. adopted the Magnitsky Rule of Accountability Act of 2012 to impose sanctions personally on Putin and named mobsters. Putin retaliated by banning adoption of Russian children by Americans. Natalia Veselnitskaya has been working for five years to repeal the Magnitsky Act. Donald Trump, Jr. reported that the meeting he, Manafort, and Kushner had with Veselnitskaya on June 9, 2016, was a dud *because she wanted to talk about adoption*. Team Trump and the Russians are using "adoption" as a code word to conflate and confuse.

The real objective of the meeting on June 9 was for the Russians to soften up Team Trump to the idea of *repealing the Magnitsky Act*. If the U.S. repeals the Magnitsky Act, Putin likely will end the ban on adoption of Russian children by Americans. President Trump praised his son for transparency. It is not transparency for Team Trump to deny Russian contacts for more than a year, and then yield details bit by bit to stay ahead of stubborn facts promised by news media.

Reality Winner.

Her name sounds like a contest. Adding the title Ms. does not change the initial reaction. Reality Winner, however, is a twenty five year old gym enthusiast, who worked in Atlanta, GA, for a contractor to the National Security Agency ("NSA"). She served six years in the U.S. Airforce, and is capable in a number of languages, including Farsi (Iran), Dari and Pashto (Afghanistan). She had access to an NSA Report that concluded the GRU (Russian Military Intelligence) hacked into VR Systems, Inc., whose software some states use for voting machines and voter registration. The Report strikes at the heart of the democratic election process. She released the Report to the Intercept, an online site that served as a platform to report on documents released by Edward Snowden. The FBI arrested Ms. Winner on a charge of Espionage, which carries an up to ten-year penalty upon conviction.

Virtual Reality in the form of a Reality Television Show Star, whom the States elected President, has met actual reality in the form of Ms. Reality Winner. The government is taking literally her threat *'to burn down the White House'*. Most Tea Party Conservatives came to Congress to figuratively burn down Washington. That is exactly the plan of Donald Trump and his acolytes Stephen Bannon and Stephen Miller. The government punishes *Leaking* severely at times in the name of National Security. The real issue is that the Executive does not want the People to know what the Executive is doing. Julius Assange and WIKI Leaks contributed to Hillary Clinton's loss of the 2016 presidential election.

Army Private First Class Bradley (now Chelsea) Manning revealed hundreds of thousands of diplomatic cables and classified Army battle reports. A Court martial sentenced Manning to thirty-five years' confinement. Before leaving office, President Obama commuted Manning's sentence to the seven years served.

President Trump has been fuming for months over leaks from his Administration holdovers from the Obama Administration and other progressives in office. He has been fighting the Russian Investigation since before he took office. Now he can vent his rage of the twenty five year old gymnast, who committed the ultimate crime in Trump's view by shining light on the attempted Russian sabotage of the 2016 presidential election. Ms. Winner's defense counsel must probe the reason for the top-secret classification of the NSA Report. Did the Report reveal sources and methods of intelligence gathering, whose disclosure could threaten the security of the Nation?

Or, did the report merely highlight the fact that Russian Military Intelligence (the GRU) tried to sabotage the 2016 election. *Why would the United States Government want to keep secret the fact that the GRU hacked into a company, whose software some states use to conduct their elections?*

The prosecution of Ms. Winner may exacerbate the strained relations between Trump and his Attorney General, Jeff Sessions, who was the first U.S. Senator to endorse Donald Trump for President. At first, it was a happy marriage. Sessions could vindicate his rejection by the Senate more than thirty years ago as a nominee for the District Court. Trump could use Sessions' strict interpretation of citizenship and immigration to promote Trump's Moslem Ban and stepped up deportation of undocumented immigrants. More importantly to Trump, he wanted to control the Department of Justice and the Russian Investigation through Sessions.

Trump's grand plan to stifle the Russian Investigation fell apart when Sessions recused himself from making decisions about the Russian Investigation. Justice Department decisions on the Russian Investigation were now in the hands of Rod Rosenstein, Deputy Attorney General, and a straight shooter.

Trump is furious about Sessions' recusal and Rosenstein's appointment of Robert Mueller as Special Counsel. Trump fired FBI Director James B. Comey on 5/9/17 because Trump was feeling the pressure of the FBI's investigation into Russian interference in the 2016 election. Despite his attempts to derail it, the FBI investigation will continue under Special Counsel Muller. Trump criticized his own Justice Department for appealing to the Supreme Court to uphold what he refers to as the "watered down" version of his proposed Moslem Ban.

Trump complained that Justice should have gone with the original version of the Ban, ignoring the fact that Trump promulgated the "watered down" version along with an Executive Order signed by Trump. Things reportedly got so testy between Sessions and Trump that Sessions allegedly offered to resign. If Trump tries to interfere or micro manage the prosecution of Ms. Reality, it may be the last straw for Attorney General Sessions. Jared Kushner reportedly urged Trump to fire FBI Director Comey, a move that blew up in Trump's face with appointment of Special Counsel Robert Mueller. Kushner's star is now on the way down in the White House.

<u>Chapter 6</u>

Trump Assault on Truth

Propaganda embraces publicity, information, hype, misinformation, and disinformation. Donald Trump is a master propagandist. He managed an election victory by winning a plurality of 80,000 votes in Wisconsin, Michigan, and Pennsylvania. His Campaign built on lies, prejudice, and Xenophobia. He gave workers in the Rust Belt the false hope that their lost jobs would come back. He has not and cannot bring those jobs back. He garnered headlines by staying a partial closure of a Carrier Indianapolis plant during the 2016 Campaign. Carrier will still move 300 blue-collar jobs to Mexico in December 2017. Trump claimed during the Campaign that he saved 1,100 jobs, but that included 300 white-collar jobs that Carrier never planned to move to Mexico.

During the 2016 Campaign, Trump used the *Little Lie* a number of times with respect to France. He had a mythical friend named 'Jim'. Jim loved France, and traveled there many times. Seeing Jim on one occasion, Trump asked, *'How is Paris or France'?* Jim answered, *'Oh, I do not go there now. Paris is not Paris any more. France is not France.'* Trump wanted to reach American voters by suggesting that France and Europe lost their countries to radical Islamic terrorism. During his trip to Paris on 7/13/17, a French reporter asked if he still felt the same way about France as his friend, Jim. Having won the election, there was no need to stress dangers of living in France or Europe from Moslems. Without blinking, Trump deflected by saying France has a 'great' and 'tough' President. The adverse propaganda morphed into cooperation.

Trump and his top people spent more than a year denying any collusion with the Russians to interfere with the 2016 election. As Jared Kushner revised his SF-86 Security Questionnaire three times, more meetings surfaced between Team Trump and the Russians. Kushner recalled a June 9, 2016 meeting with a Russian attorney to obtain something about Hillary Clinton. On the 7/7/17 return flight on Airforce One from the G20 meeting in Hamburg, Trump attorneys (and possibly the President) cooked up a story to cover Donald Trump, Jr.'s meeting with the Russian attorney.

The first story Don, Jr., released was that the Russian attorney raised only the subject of American adoption of Russian children. The New York Times, however, was on the story and Team Trump had to correct their reality distortion field slightly. Don, Jr., admitted that he thought the Russian attorney had something that would help the Trump Campaign. Competing power centers within the White House kept leaking to the New York Times, which informed Don, Jr., of the paper's plan to release the chain of emails that told the story of Team Trump's meeting with the Russian Lawyer. Donald Trump, Jr. suddenly became as transparent as a Macy's window display.

One hour before the Times ran the story, Don Jr. released the emails from Rob Goldstone, the music publicist for Emin Agaralov, son of Russian oligarch Aras Agaralov. In 2013, Donald Trump took his Miss Universe Pageant to Agaralov's Crocus City Hall in Moscow. While there, he became good friends with both Agaralovs and Rob Goldstone. Trump planned to build a Trump Tower in Moscow with Aras Agaralov's help. It did not hurt the relationship that Aras Agaralov was in the circle of Vladimir Putin's moneyed Russian Oligarchs.

Goldstone-Don, Jr. Emails

The Goldstone emails promised compromising information on Hillary Clinton coming from the State Prosecutors Office in Moscow. Don Jr. replied that if it is what you say, *'I love it'*. This looks awfully like a conspiracy to violate U.S. Campaign Finance Law, which prohibits taking money or *'anything of value'* from a foreign source. After a year of dishonest denials of Russian collusion, President Trump praised his son for transparency (forced by the New York Times), and claimed, *'It was Opposition Research'*. According to the President, *'Most people would have taken the meeting'*.

Master of Deflection.

Sometimes President Trump avoids the *Big Lie* and the *Little Lie*, and simply deflects or conflates facts and issues. Reporters asked the President if it was wrong for his son Donald to take the meeting with the Russian attorney. Trump shot back that the Russian attorney was in the United States at the time reportedly *on a visa signed by Attorney General Loretta Lynch*. The visa was not the issue. Trump wanted to change the subject. The issue was Team Trump's collusion with the Russians to interfere with the U.S. election.

Former KGB Spy.

The Russian attorney showed up on June 9, 2016, at the meeting with Jared Kushner, Don, Jr., and Paul Manafort, with a former KGB spy in tow. According to the Associated Press, the former Intelligence Office, Rinat Akhmetshin is now a lobbyist. The President has already set up the answer to this minor detail. According to the President, the meeting was brief. One of the Team Trump players allegedly left the meeting *almost immediately*. The other Team Trump Player allegedly *did not focus* on the meeting [or the danger presented to U.S. National Security]. Team Trump Party Line: *'Nobody here but us chickens, and we're not talking.'*

White House Divided.

No house can stand divided against itself. This holds true for the White House, which is coming apart at the seams as different power centers jockey for the seat behind the throne. Stephen Bannon and Stephen Miller initially rose to power by cobbling together a policy that mesmerized White Working Class voters by attacking Elites, Europe, Iranians, Mexicans, Moslems, Migrants, and NATO. After the election, power shifted to Jared Kushner and Ivanka Kushner, the President's daughter, who advocated moderation. Jared became plenipotentiary empowered by the president to resolve tensions in the Middle East, and the President's Ambassador in general to the World. Secretary of State Tillerson could languish at the margins.

SF 86 Hand Grenade.

Remember the meeting of Team Trump with the Russian attorney to get the goods on Hillary Clinton. Of the three Trump managers present, Jared Kushner was the only one employed by the Government and, because he advised the president on top-secret matters, he had to complete Standard Form 86, the Security Questionnaire under oath. Kushner initially averred that he never had any meetings with foreign nationals. His lawyers learned, possibly through leaks to the New York Times from the Bannon-Miller faction, that Team Trump had meetings with Russians. Kushner amended his SF86 three times to include a long list of foreign nationals, including Natalia Veselnitskaya (the Russian lady attorney with the goods on Hillary), Sergey Kislyak (the Russian Ambassador), and Sergey Gorkov (President of VEB Russia State Bank, a graduate of FSB Spy School, and friend of Vladimir Putin).

Power Centers Explode.

Despite what he sometimes says, President Trump does not hold transparency as a virtue. Kushner's transparency is making the *Big Lie,* about no collusion with the Russians, look like, well, a *Big Lie*. Kushner's candor is forcing an uncomfortable transparency on Don Jr., the President's son. It looks as though Kushner's rising star has fallen. The White House is in chaos as result of the cover-up of collusion with the Russians in interfering with the 2016 election. Team Trump tried a year of denials, aided and abetted by GOP surrogates who parroted the *Party Line* that the Russian investigation was a witch-hunt.

When the *Big Lie* failed to stop the investigation, President Trump fired the FBI Director for missteps in the investigation of Hillary Clinton's lapse of security in handling State Department emails. Trump emulated President Nixon by first asking Dan Coats, Director of National Intelligence, and Mike Pompeo, CIA Director, to suggest to FBI Director Comey that the Russia investigation could hurt National Security. Nixon asked CIA Director Richard Helms to inform the FBI that disclosure of hush money to cover up the Watergate Burglary would hurt National Security. Chief Executives often subvert the Nation on pretext of National Security.

Kushner Urges Firing Comey.

The end of the Jared-Ivanka power center came as result of Jared Kushner's advising Trump to fire FBI Director Comey. Why would Kushner urge the President to fire the FBI Director on a pretext? It must have occurred to someone in the White House that Comey's firing would appear to be a clumsy attempt to stop the Russia investigation. The most likely explanation is that Kushner also felt the heat from the FBI investigation. Kushner (born January 10, 1981) cold have no memory of the Saturday Night Massacre, when Nixon fired Special Prosecutor Archibald Cox on October 20, 1973. If Kushner, Donald Trump, and Don Jr., felt the heat from Comey's investigation, that heat should intensify under Special Counsel Mueller.

Robert Mueller has power to investigate collusion with Russian interference, to empanel a federal grand jury, to seek criminal indictments, and to prosecute anyone who aided Russia or conspired with Russia to interfere with the 2016 presidential election. Mueller is empowered to exercise powers of the FBI, the Department of Justice, and Office of U.S. Attorney.

No President Pence.

Vice President Mike Pence is starting to distance himself from Team Trump. Pence issued a statement that, *'He was not aware of the meeting* [with the Russian lady attorney]. *He is also not focused on stories about the campaign—especially those pertaining to the time before he joined the campaign.'* Curiously, Pence is reluctant to issue a broad denial that he never met with any Russians. When questioned about any Pence meeting with any Russians, Pence's Press Spokesperson, Marc Lotter deflected. The Vice President is *'working on the agenda the American People sent him to Washington to accomplish'*.

If Trump goes by resignation or impeachment, Pence has to precede Trump out the door, just as Spiro Agnew departed before Nixon resigned. Pence has not definitively denied any meetings with Russians or other foreign nationals who might be interested in interfering with the 2016 election. At all events, Pence was an enabler. He never criticized Trump, no matter Trump's un-American comments and proposed policies to single out Moslems and migrants. When the *Access Hollywood* Bus Tapes aired October 7, 2016, and disclosed Trump's groping syndrome, Pence choked shortly until the Obama Administration announced Russian interference with the 2016 election on the same day. To avoid political interference, neither Obama nor Comey signed the Statement.

Putin's Soul.

George W. Bush looked into Vladimir Putin's eyes and saw his soul. Bush found Putin *"straight forward and trustworthy"*, which likely drew a chuckle from the former KGB Colonel. President Obama found Putin the aggressor in invading Ukraine, taking Crimea, and subverting eastern Ukraine. Obama applied sanctions, including freezing the Exxon Mobil contract to bring American technology to develop Russia's petroleum reserves. Donald Trump the candidate was more or less pro Putin. *"Wouldn't it be nice if we got along with Russia"?* There were rumors that Russians invested millions of dollars in the Trump Organization. Seventeen U.S. intelligence agencies concluded that Russia hacked the Democratic Party computers and interfered with the US. 2016 Presidential election.

Trump had to fire National Security Adviser Lt. Gen. (Ret.) Michael Flynn for lying about discussions with Russian Ambassador Sergey Kislyak to lift sanctions.

The House, Senate, and FBI are investigating. Trump was concerned that FBI Director James B. Comey would not express personal loyalty to Trump or let go of the investigation against sacked Security Advisor Flynn. The topic of Russia is now toxic. Team Trump no longer brags about Russians investing millions into the Trump Organization. Trump and son Eric are careful how they speak of Russia. *"We have no projects there."* Like the dog in the night that is mysteriously missing, the Trumps never say that Russians did not invest money in the Trump Organization or that Russians do not hold any mortgages on Trump properties. The investigators need to see Donald Trump's tax returns.

According to Vanity Fair, Tina Nguyen byline 5/8/17, Eric Trump told golf writer James Dodson that the Russians invested millions of dollars in the Trump Organization. *"We have all the funding we need out of Russia."* Eric Trump calls the story a complete fabrication and "an example of why there is such distrust of the media in our country".

Chapter 7

Facts Are Stubborn Things That Do Not Go Away.

"Facts are stubborn things; and whatever may be our wishes, our inclinations, or the dictates of our passions, they cannot alter the state of facts and evidence." John Adams.

President Trump longs for the virtual reality formerly enjoyed by businessperson Donald Trump in another life, where he wrote the script and determined the outcome of the show. For seven seasons, Trump acted out his fantasies on his own television show, *The Apprentice*. The highlight of the shows came when Trump simply said, *'You're Fired'* to the unlucky individual Trump decided was unworthy of remaining in the Trump spotlight. There is a bit of the sadist in Donald Trump. Do not misunderstand. It is not about inflicting pain. Conventional wisdom is that sadists enjoy hurting others. The hurt, however, is a byproduct. *The essence of sadism is control*. Trump can manage and even fire his Cabinet as president, but he wants to bring control of events even closer to home, so he can have direct influence over what happens in his presidency.

Trump has a Vice President, Mike Pence, who is a mainstream conservative Republican. The Vice President, however, is a constitutional officer, the one person on the Trump Team, whom Trump cannot fire.

That is why Trump casually tossed, as if over his shoulder, the portfolio for resolution of problems in Israel, Palestine, and the Middle East to his 36-year-old son in law, Jared Kushner. Jared and Donald will resolve emergent issues in the Middle East (and likely Europe and Asia) at dinner over blintzes or schnitzel. There is no need to clutter the agenda or the discussion with the presence of constitutional officers or cabinet secretaries. Trump wants to run the Government like a sole proprietor of a mom and pop business. Does anyone doubt but that in a discussion with his son in law, Trump will have the last word. As President, Trump would have the last word. It is smoother, however, to have it *'All in the Family'*.

Dan Fried, former Obama State Department official disclosed 6/1/17 that the Trump Administration fought to lift sanctions on Russia as soon as Trump took the oath of office. The State Department dragged its heels. Fried and others notified Congress about Trump's attempt to lift Russian sanctions. Senator Lindsey Graham and Congressman Adam Schiff introduced legislation to require approval of Congress to lift sanctions. Trump's son in law Jared Kushner acquired 666 Fifth Avenue on a $1.2 billion two-year note, which Kushner desperately needs to refinance. Kushner met with Russian Bank VEB and with Sergey Gorkov, a Russian Billionaire to look for financing. Russian Ambassador Sergey Kislyak suggested the meeting with Gorkov. Team Trump claims that the meetings with the Russians were to arrange for cooperation with Russian military to defeat terror groups in Syria. The Russians, however, support the largest terror group in Syria, Bashar al Assad's Government.

Trump wants to cut the budget of the State Department by twenty five percent. In Trump's opinion, the State Department is too independent and not helpful. To take the heat off Trump, Rex Tillerson, former head of Exxon Mobil, will take care of Russia, including bringing Exxon

Mobil technology to develop Russia's vast petroleum reserves, after Trump lifts sanctions imposed by President Obama. Trump and Kushner will take care of the rest of the world. Trump wants to increase the budget of the Defense Department by Fifty Billion Dollars. Defense Secretary, General (Ret.) Mattis, was of the opinion that the cuts in State would require Defense to buy more bullets, on the rationale that State can exert policy influence more easily than can infantry.

Trump's long-running feud with the media is the direct result of the media obsession with publishing facts. Newspapers and talk shows sometimes deal in rumors and false reports, which in most cases are ultimately resolved as facts. As an entrepreneur and playboy in Manhattan, Trump was the target of many stories and rumors. At the end of the day, many of the stories were true. He did marry three wives after tidying up with two divorces. He was married to Ivana, then to Marla Maples, and now to Melania. What bothered Trump was that he could not control the media or the stories. It was often inconvenient for Trump, married or engaged to one woman, to see a story about him allegedly seen with another woman.

No president in the history of the U.S. started his term with worse relations with the press than did Trump. He knows there are stubborn facts out there that will not go away. He knows that the media will report those facts to the American People. If the message is hostile because it is true, kill the messenger. In Trump's case, he tried to delegitimize the media by claiming that the news was fake news. This worked wonders with Trump's Base. The public, however, does not believe Trump. Sixty-one percent think Trump fired FBI Director James B. Comey to protect Trump. Only thirty-four percent feel Trump is doing a good job as President.

Fired FBI Head Comey Goes Public Before Senate Intelligence Committee.

At a hearing before the Senate Intelligence Committee on June 8, 2017, Comey explained that he documented his meetings with President Trump because he feared Trump would lie about the substance of their discussion. Comey confirmed that Trump asked him to let go of the investigation into the Russian connection of Lt. Gen. (Ret.) Michael Flynn, the National Security Adviser Trump fired after twenty-four days in office. Ironically, Comey testified that Trump was not under investigation while Comey was Head of the FBI.

Special Counsel Robert Mueller will investigate Trump actions and statements. That will show that Trump, in his own words, felt pressure from the FBI Russian Investigation. Trump hoped Comey would let go of the Flynn investigation, and asked Comey to maintain personal loyalty to Trump. Trump dangled Comey's job as an inducement to maintain personal loyalty to

Trump. He felt relieved from pressure of the FBI Investigation after firing Comey; and likely lied when he stated that he never asked Comey to let go of the Flynn investigation.

Marc Kasowitz, the lawyer who guided N.J. Governor Chris Christie through the Bridge Gate scandal and investigation, now represents trump. The criticism over Comey's firing may force Trump to change his ways. He could stop sending out tweets and stop lying to the American People. Trump announced his appointment of Christopher Wray to Head the FBI. Kasowitz solemnly announced that Trump did not ask Comey to let go of the Russian Investigation. Trump's first Campaign Manager, Corey Lewandoski, proclaimed that Trump was telling the truth and that Comey was lying. Trump will now reprise a modern version of the tragic events of the sixteenth century, where Henry VIII and his acolytes tried in vain to invent their own facts. Deputy Press Secretary Sara Huckabee Sanders announced that Trump is not a liar, reminiscent of Richard Nixon's plea of, *'I am not a crook'*.

Special Dilemma of Special Counsel Robert Mueller

As Special Counsel, Robert Mueller has broad investigative power. He can employ the FBI to investigate. He can convene a grand jury to hand up criminal indictments. He can prosecute crimes in federal court. As former Director of the FBI, Mueller does not want to turn his artillery on fellow former FBI Director James Comey. After several meetings with Trump, Comey wrote memos to document the unusual substance of his alleged conversations with Trump, and presidential interference with FBI investigations. Comey leaked the substance of those memos indirectly to the New York Times through a Columbia law Professor. Trump and his lawyer, Marc Kasowitz, have already labelled Comey "a leaker". Most leaks prosecute under the Espionage Act. Comey carefully kept his memos on Trump free of Classified Information.

Mueller, therefore, should not have a case against Comey under the Espionage Act. Ironically, the Executive Branch hands out classified status. Team Trump might classify Comey's memos after the fact to try to make Mueller's job difficult.

Eventually, Mueller will seek to have President Trump answer questions under oath. *Who will Bell the Cat?* Presidents are immune from normal process. An aggrieved person can file a civil suit against a sitting president, as President Clinton discovered in the Paula Jones sexual harassment case. Special Counsel Mueller, however, cannot bring an indictment against Trump based on perjury without having the President lie under oath. It is not clear that a Special Counsel can bring a criminal case against a sitting president. If Special Counsel Mueller notices Trump's deposition, the President might just ignore the Notice of Deposition. The Constitution provides for Impeachment of a president by a simple majority on each ground set forth as a separate Article of Impeachment.

Articles of Impeachment are merely an accusation or indictment. The Chief Justice will preside over trial with one hundred Senators acting as jurors and as arbiter of disputes on process and admission of evidence. Removal of the President will result only if two thirds of Senators present agree with one of more Articles of Impeachment. House Managers act as Prosecutors.

As usual, Speaker of the House and second in line for succession to the presidency, Paul Ryan, excused Trump's attempted corruption of government as the innocent work of someone not familiar with the protocols of government. Ryan's protection of Trump may soon cost him his seat. Ryan cannot win in November 2018 by carrying only Trump's Base, which is down to thirty-four percent of the vote. A steelworker named Randy Bryce announced his run for Ryan's seat in November 2018. Ryan's sponsorship of the bare bones American Health Care Act may be enough to put Bryce in office.

Armed & Dangerous Fringe.

On 6/14/17, Republican Members of Congress practiced baseball to prepare for the annual charity game with the Democrats. A lunatic with an assault rifle shattered the early morning calm by attacking the GOP ballplayers. The first shot was mistaken for a car backfire. As the gunman fired multiple shots into the men on the ballfield, they realized that they were under lethal assault. Steve Scalise (LA), Majority Whip, was playing second base. The gunman shot Scalise in the hip, inflicting critical injuries, which required multiple surgeries and blood transfusions. Because Scalise had a leadership position, two Capitol Police Officers engaged the gunman at the scene. Together with arriving Alexandria, VA, police, they neutralized the gunman, who expired. The gunman had a history of business failure and simmering resentment of those who prospered. Before he fired the first shot, he casually asked one of the departing Congressmen if the players were Democrats or Republicans. The shooter was a volunteer for Bernie Sanders in 2016. Sanders condemned the shootings.

Tone Down Whose Rhetoric?

Voices call out on both sides of the aisle to tone down the rhetoric of political debate. On 6/1/5/17, House Minority Leader Nancy Pelosi said, *'It does not have be this way.'* She went on to note that Members of Congress got along until the 1990s, when the Republicans started 'their politics of personal destruction'. In 1994, Republicans took control of the House of Representatives after thirty-four years in the wilderness. They elected Newt Gingrich Speaker and adopted their manifesto, *Contract for America*. The tone in Washington changed. Collegiality between the two major political parties became a distant memory, recalled by the occasional cooperation and personal affection between President Ronald Reagan and Speaker Tip O'Neil in the 1980s. The personal profile of House Members changed. The newly minted GOP Members did not see themselves as part of the Capital Establishment, which is positive.

The negative is that they tended to keep their families in their home districts. Many of them stayed with other GOP Members in bachelor pads in and around Washington. Fraternization with their political opponents was for the most part not on their agenda. They and their Tea Party successors came to Washington, not to glorify it, but to figuratively burn it down. Ironically, the Trump Justice Department appears ready to charge leaker Reality Winner with terrorism because she talked of burning down Washington. The new Republican Party considers Democrats to be the enemy. For Republicans, it is the *party line* to not even refer to the Democratic Party. GOP Talking Points insist that the proper name for their opponents is the *Democrat* Party. The word *'Democratic'* to describe their opponents is taboo to the GOP because it signifies support of the People, the *Demos*.

The 2016 presidential campaign was not a model of civility. Candidate Trump promised (as if he were a tin pot dictator of a banana republic) that, if elected, he would send Hillary Clinton to prison. Trump started his campaign in 2011 with the *Big Lie* that Barack Obama was not born in the U.S., and, therefore ineligible to be President. He maintained and reaffirmed the *Big Lie* repeatedly through 2016, when he simply walked away from what he knew from the start was deceitful, because it was no longer profitable. The Office of President requires respect. Personal failings of the incumbent should not detract from the office. It is becoming impossible, however, to ignore the narcissism, incoherence, vindictiveness, guilt complex—as to his legitimacy and possible collusion of his Campaign with Russian interference in the 2016 election—and pervasive conflicts of interest of President Donald John Trump and the Trump Organization.

To demand respect and civility, Trump must practice what he preaches. Trump made a formal visit to the Supreme Court 6/15/17 to welcome installation of his appointee and newest Justice, Neil M. Gorsuch. Trump, however, has made derisive remarks about Court members. He has referred to Chief Justice John G. Roberts as *'an absolute disaster,'* presumably for upholding Obamacare twice. As to Justice Ruth Bader Ginsburg, he previously claimed, *'her mind is shot'*.

Chapter 8

Trump Denies Russian Computer Hacking.

Here is a question to highlight the stark reality of the massive cyber-attack Russia launched against the United States in 2015-2016. *Did you know that the Democratic National Committee* (DNC) *computer was streaming data on line to Moscow?* How could that happen? Russia has a number of rogue computer hacking groups, including *Fancy Bear, Cozy Bear*, and *Guccifer 2.0 (a handle used by GRU, Russia Military Intelligence, and FSB)*, all of which carry out computer cyberwarfare operations on behalf of the Russian Government. Russian hackers pen-etrated and took over DNC computers. Russians took over the computer of John Podesta, Man-ager of Hillary's Campaign, through *spear-phishing*, a Trojan-Horse email. The email cautioned that an intruder gained access to Podesta's password.

Podesta's office forwarded the email to their security firm, which identified it as legitimate (later saying it meant illegitimate). Podesta's office replied to the effect of, *Thanks, here is our new password*. The Russians were in. FBI warned DNC in 2105 that Russians were hacking DNC computers. FBI, however, left multiple messages on DNC website help desk, and did not alert senior DNC staff of Russian cyberattacks. DNC computer technician had their security firm look for hacks, but the firm did not find any breach. Other FBI warnings left at help desk did not alert DNC senior staff until the damage was beyond repair.

Trump Campaign Collusion?

The answer to collusion is that the Trump Campaign was delighted that Russian hackers re-leased embarrassing emails from computers of DNC and Podesta. Trump announced, *'Russia, if you're listening, I hope you are able to find the 30,000 [Hillary] emails that are missing'*. Roger Stone, Trump's adviser, claimed he was in contact with WikiLeaks just before they released emails to sabotage the Campaign of Hillary Clinton. Candidate Trump also said, *'I love Wik-iLeaks'*. It is beyond dispute that candidate Trump and the Trump Campaign wanted Russian hackers and WikiLeaks to continue to help bring down Hillary Clinton's Campaign. These facts will not go away. For President Trump to admit Russian hacking means that he admits he is il-legitimate. He must disparage his own Intelligence Agencies instead of the Russians.

Few presidents started their terms in office with greater hostility towards their own Intelligence Agencies than did President Trump. The CIA must have been puzzled because they have one client only, the President of the United States. How do we know candidate Trump was not happy with the CIA? Whenever the media or the press would refer to CIA intelligence that was anything but praiseful of candidate Trump, he would sound off that, *'These are the same people who promised there were Weapons of Mass Destruction (WMD) in Iraq.'*

It was an integral part of Trump Campaign policy to denigrate U.S. Intelligence Agencies. Vladimir Putin must have been smiling, because it was all about Russia. The CIA and the FBI were investigating Russian interference in the 2016 election and possible collusion between the Russians and members of the Trump Campaign.

Trump could not tolerate the Russian investigation because it called his patriotism into question. More importantly to him, the investigation called his legitimacy as president into question. Trump fought back as he always does, by attacking the *bona fides* of his critics. Many do not understand that Trump is a master of propaganda. He destroyed the presidential aspirations of Jeb Bush, the odds on favorite to win the GOP nomination in 2016, with two words, *'Low Energy'*. He finished off his other primary opponents, Senators Rubio and Cruz, with *'Little Marco'*, and *'Lyin' Ted'*. He won the general election with *'Crooked Hillary'*. No propagandist in history has been more successful than is Donald Trump. His timing is impeccable. His use of social media, including *Twitter*, allows him to keep in touch with his Base.

If someone were to complain that calling Hillary Clinton a crook is over the top and beyond the pale, he could use a truth to conflate and confuse critics. He could say, *'The FBI has been investigating Hillary for the past year.'* For good measure, Trump saddled Hillary with the idea that she had to take a nap after every campaign event.

Trump's *'nap attack'* on Hillary was not an example of the *Big Lie* (*Grosse Lüge*). It may or may not have been a *Little Lie*. For the U.S. Intelligence Agencies, Trump did not need to employ the *Big Lie*. Trump beat down the Intelligence Agencies with the truth. The CIA badly botched the investigation of possible WMD in Iraq. The CIA abandoned its primary mission, to collect and report facts, and became a tool of the political policies of the Bush Cheney Administration. Scooter Libby, Cheney's Chief of Staff, and Vice President Cheney made several trips to CIA Headquarters in Langley, Virginia. Libby and Cheney instructed CIA analysts to make a finding of WMD in Iraq. CIA Director George Tenet promised President Bush that finding WMD in Iraq in 2003 was a *'Slam Dunk'*.

Ambassador Joseph Wilson debunked the rumor that Saddam Hussein accessed yellowcake uranium from Niger. Cheney inspired Libby, Deputy Chief of Staff Karl Rove, Deputy Secretary of State Richard Armitage and others to unmask Valerie Plame, Wilson's wife, as a covert CIA Agent in violation of the *Intelligence Identities Protection Act of 1982*.

Bush needed WMD in Iraq to justify the Invasion. Nuclear weapons were part of the WMD party line. Ambassador Wilson wrote an Op Ed in the New York Times 7/6/03, *'What I Didn't Find in Africa.* By outing Wilson's wife as a CIA Agent, Cheney suggested that Wilson's wife sent him to Niger on a junket. Acting Attorney General James B. Comey appointed Patrick Fitzgerald Special Counsel to look for violation of intelligence law. A trial jury convicted Scooter Libby of perjury. Karl Rove walked away after *five appearances* before the grand jury. Bush commuted Libby's prison sentence but refused to pardon him. Cheney was furious, and never had as much influence in the Bush Administration after the Libby conviction.

Bush was fixated on invading Iraq, but he desperately needed the CIA to confirm existence of WMD as a justification for the Iraq War. George Tenet gave Bush the cover he needed to launch the War. The CIA sent a team of investigators to Iraq after the war to search for WMD. David Kay headed the team, which searched diligently. There were no WMD found in Iraq. George Tenet had to resign. When Donald Trump mentioned WMD in 2016, he knew it would discredit the CIA and help to defuse reports of CIA investigation of Russian interference in the 2016 election. For the FBI, Trump used the personal approach. He spoke with FBI Director Comey. He had a private dinner with Comey to see if Comey would like to cooperate with Trump. He suggested that Comey let go of the investigation into Lt. Gen. (Ret.) Mike Flynn, his sacked Security Advisor.

When Comey demonstrated that he would continue the Russian investigation, Trump dismissed him. Trump asked Attorney General Sessions and Deputy Attorney General Rod Rosenstein to justify Comey's termination. To maintain Justice Department integrity, Rosenstein appointed former FBI Chief Robert Mueller Special Counsel to manage the Russian investigation. Rosenstein acted because Sessions, as a Trump Campaign Surrogate, recused himself from involvement in the Russian investigation. The President was furious. He had lost control of the Justice Department. A few days later, a friend of Trump casually announced that Trump was considering firing Special Counsel Mueller. The White House denied that the friend was speaking for the President. The master propagandist had struck again, by firing a shot across the bow. Mueller had better think twice before crossing Trump.

Like all tin pot dictators, Trump insists on his version of the facts. He denigrates the media and the press because he knows that ultimately they will disseminate the facts, which frequently will be adverse to him as President. He lampooned the U.S. intelligence agencies because they unanimously concluded that Russia interfered with the U.S. Presidential election in 2016. He cannot look at Russian interference and be concerned about a foreign power threatening our democratic Republic. He can see only a threat to his crumbling ego. Hillary could not have won the popular vote by nearly three million. Clinton's plurality must have come from illegal aliens in California and New York.

His twitterstorms are desperate gasps of exhaustion, fear, pride, and anger. He must remove all traces of President Obama from the nation's records. He must repeal Obamacare, because he promised to do so. To obscure the public opposition to the GOP Healthcare Bill, he issued a warning to Syria about planned U.S. retaliation for a poison gas attack that he imagined might be imminent. He fired the FBI Director because he feared the Russia Investigation. He called into question the impartiality of Special Counsel Robert Mueller because he still fears the Russia Investigation. He trapped himself in a Greek Tragedy where Donald Trump fancies himself as hero, Trump's *hoi polloi* see him as the strong Nationalist Leader, but the educated fear he may be *The Manchurian Candidate.*

G20 Conference.

Trump attended the G20 Conference in Hamburg, Germany, on July 6-9, 2017.He was no longer the leader of the free world. Angela Merkel, Chancellor of Germany, opined a month earlier that Europe could no longer rely on the U.S. Trump walked away from the Paris Climate Accord. He was anti-immigrant. His policy on trade was America first. He considered NATO obsolete. He dragged chis feet on affirming the NATO Article 5 Mutual Defense Pact. The script could not be better for Russia, if Putin had written it. Trump painted himself into a corner with respect to Russian hacking. If Trump was uncertain of the identity of the enemy who made the cyberattack on the U.S., why should Putin be anxious? Trump publically stated that he was not sure who attacked our democracy. According to Trump, a four hundred pound guy sitting on a bed may have made the cyberattack.

Closed Meeting Helps Russia.

Trump and Putin met at Hamburg on 7/7/17. Who wrote the script, Trump or Putin? The media and press were not present, except for preliminary photos. Aside from translators, the only persons present were Trump, Putin, Tillerson (US Secretary of State), and Lavrov (Russia

Foreign Minister).There were no note takers. Gen. (Ret.) H.R. McMaster (U.S. National Security Adviser) was not invited. Trump brought up the issue of Russian hacking. Putin denied Russian involvement. According to Tillerson's post meeting debrief, the U.S effectively capitulated by agreeing to move on from the intractable issue of the Russian cyberattack. If Trump continues with his plan to lift sanctions on Russia, Putin's triumph will be complete.

Tillerson touted *'positive chemistry'* between Trump and Putin at the 2017 G20. Since Putin has taken Team Trump for fools and amateurs since 2015, Putin doubtless is beaming with positive vibes. Putin has a naval supply base on the Syrian coast, so he wants to save the regime of Bashar al Assad. U.S. Syrian policy is nebulous. Putin needed Sevastopol for a homeport for Russia's Navy, so he invaded Crimea. President Obama imposed economic sanctions, which Trump wants to lift. Putin sent Russian troops without insignia to destabilize eastern Ukraine and to maintain a Russian controlled land corridor to Sevastopol. Team Trump is busy investigating the 2016 election, but only to try to prove Trump won the popular vote.

Putin orchestrated a massive hack of the computers of the DNC and John Podesta, Hillary Clinton's 2016 Campaign Manager. Putin gladly used the services of WikiLeaks to release thousands of emails stolen from the DNC and Podesta's office. Trump colluded by saying, *'Russia, if you're listening, I hope you find the 30,000 emails that are missing.'* Trump is not sure if the Russians interfered in the U.S. election. *'It might have been a 400 pound guy sitting on a bed.'* Rex Tillerson saw *'positive chemistry'* in the Putin-Trump exchange. Never has Putin been able to gain so much in exchange for a smile.

It must be Putin, who is writing the script. Hillary Clinton had a strong position against Russian aggression. In 2011, Hillary kept the pressure on during Russia's civil unrest. Putin had to struggle to get through his 2012 election. He vowed to do all he could to keep Hillary from the White House. Russia's intelligence services agreed that Russia could be more expansive and dominant under Donald trump than under Hillary Clinton. As a former Lt. Col., in the KGB, Putin respects Russia's intelligence services. Trump is at war with his Intelligence Services because they rightly reported Russia's hacking of the 2015-2016 election. Trump appointed Kris Kobach, a known vote suppressor, Co-chair of the Election Integrity Commission to find the imagined three million aliens who denied Trump the popular vote.

Trump's relation with Russia is an unfair match. Putin supports his intelligence services. Trump is afraid his intelligence services will show him as an illegitimate president because of Russian hacking. CIA covers overseas intelligence. FBI covers domestic counterespionage.

Trump rewarded the FBI by firing its Director on a pretext of mistakes in the investigation of email procedures used by Hillary Clinton. Trump rewarded CIA by continually mocking its finding of WMD in Iraq nearly *fifteen* years ago. Trump is hobbling CIA, FBI, and State Department. Trump mistakenly believes that his legitimacy as president requires him to discredit his own Intelligence Agencies.

Trump Tweet 7:50 AM 7/9/17. *"Putin & I discussed forming an impenetrable Cyber Security unit so that election hacking & many other negative things will be guarded."* U.S. Treasury Secretary Steve Mnuchin thought that would be a great idea. Senator John McCain noted that the Russians know a lot about computer hacking. After everyone but Steve Mnuchin trashed the idea of collaborating with the Russians on computer security, Trump abandoned the idea by tweet thirteen hours later.

Chapter 9

Little Marco, Lyin' Ted, & Crooked Hillary

In 2015-2016, Donald Trump waged a cynical campaign calculated to appeal to xenophobia and racial and religious prejudices. After making a theatrical descent on Fifth Avenue's Trump Tower elevator, Trump disclosed Mexicans and Mexico as his first scapegoats. His first promise, to build a wall along the U.S. southwest border to deny entry to Mexicans. Ironically, the movement of Mexican Nationals along the U.S. border generally headed in a southerly direction since the recession of 2008. As a dividend, Trump promised that Mexico would pay for the wall, knowing that no president of Mexico could agree to pay for the wall. The border wall was a deceitful, empty promise because Trump knew he would never build the wall. Trump's next target was Moslems. Trump promised to halt entry of Moslems into the U.S. He promised to exclude Moslems multiple times during the campaign.

U.S. Courts struck down his Executive Orders banning entry of Moslems from six majority Moslem countries that coincidentally have little or no Trump Family business. On the second go around of the Moslem Ban, Trump removed Iraq from the list of banned countries. The U.S. has a large military presence in Iraq and needs support of Iraqi translators, who need a safe haven after public disclosure of their collaboration with the U.S. Trump claimed the danger shown by the 9/11/01 attack required a Moslem ban. Afghanistan, Egypt, and Saudi Arabia had the most immediate connection with the 9/11 attack, but were omitted from the ban list. The Trump family has businesses or plans to do business in Egypt and Saudi Arabia. Attorneys for the U.S. Justice Department are asking Courts in 2017 to ignore President Trump's campaign promises to ban Moslems. It seems that a bit of the man and his campaign have rubbed off on the office of president and his Executive Orders.

Trump Advisor Stephen Miller appeared on TV to resolve the challenges to Trump's Executive Orders implementing the Moslem Travel Ban. Miller has no legal training, no understanding of the Constitution, and no knowledge of the limits of presidential power. According to Miller, President Trump has last word on immigration and travel issues. Miller claimed that Trump's Executive Orders on the Moslem Travel Ban are not reviewable by the Courts. Trump praised Miller for his loyalty and conviction, and likely resolved never to allow Miller to speak for the Administration again. A handful of Courts, including Courts of Appeal, ruled against the Moslem Ban. The U.S. Supreme Court will decide the issue.

Trump laid the groundwork for the 2015-2016 campaign as far back as 2011, when he promoted himself as *Birther in Chief*. The Birther Movement was a campaign by the Republican Base to delegitimize President Obama by claiming that he was not a native-born U.S. citizen, and, therefore, ineligible under the Constitution to be president. Trump had two main objectives in claiming President Obama was not born in the U.S. First, an attack on the legitimacy of President Obama would rally the Republican Base behind Trump. Second, the smear would be an indirect attack on Hillary Clinton, the presumptive favorite of President Obama in the 2016 race. Trump's Birther strategy depended on a lie that Trump knew was a lie. To breathe virtual truth into his lie, Trump played a charade. Trump announced that he sent detectives to Honolulu to report the truth. No report ever came out.

In 2016, Trump announced without apology or explanation that President Obama was born in the U.S. He blamed the birther conspiracy, without any evidence, on rumors allegedly started by Hillary Clinton's 2008 primary campaign against Barack Obama. Trump operates in a fact free virtual world, similar to his former reality show, *'The Apprentice'*. Trump and his two Oval Office Apprentices, Stephen Bannon and Steven Miller, push the envelope to gauge how much reality distortion the American People, or, more importantly, Trump's *hoi polloi* are willing to accept as at least plausible. It is astonishing how much support Team Trump can garner from anti Obama rhetoric, whether on healthcare, energy, climate, or federal regulations.

Campaign by Insult.

Trump lowered the level of his campaign to reach his base supporters. He spoke on a level that a fifth grader would understand. He attacked his opponents personally. Jeb Bush, former Governor of Florida and a contender for the GOP nomination in 2016, never recovered from

Trump's description of Jeb as *'Low Energy'*. Trump quickly won over to his camp the support of competitors like Chris Christie, Governor of New Jersey, former House Speaker Newt Gingrich, and former Mayor of New York, Rudy Giuliani. At first, Trump and Texas Senator Ted Cruz ignored each other. Cruz' strategy was to allow Trump to implode, and to position Cruz to pick up the majority of Trump supporters. This required Cruz to show respect for Trump, and not alienate Trump supporters. Trump decided that he had to stop Cruz after Cruz won the Iowa Caucus in February. Trump started referring to Cruz as 'Lyin' Ted' in March.

Relying on a National Enquirer photo, Trump asked why Ted Cruz' father appeared in a scene with Lee Harvey Oswald, assassin of President Kennedy. In turn, Cruz dismissed Trump as a pathological liar. Trump dismissed Florida Senator Rubio as *'Little Marco'*. Trump attacked Secretary Clinton as *'Crooked 'Hillary'*. The Republican base loved it. No criticism stuck to Trump, who gave new meaning to the Reagan descriptor *Teflon Candidate*. Trump insulated himself by holding friendship with David Pecker, Chief Executive of *The National Enquirer*. Trump fared better with the tabloid than other candidates. He never apologized and never showed shame, the quality that makes normal people vulnerable.

Chapter 10

Impeachment Remedy for Dereliction of Duty.

Before elected President, Trump thought the Office of President was a cakewalk. Ironically, no one believed the voters would elect Trump President. Trump did not imagine he would win. That is why he claimed the system is rigged. *He carefully laid the foundation for an expected loss a year before the election to save loss of face*. Trump kept chattering about a rigged system until Election Day. He could not bear the thought of Hillary Clinton beating him. Trump's Campaign team thought he would lose. New Jersey Governor Chris Christie headed the Campaign Transition Team, which, assuming a loss, did nothing to recruit anyone to serve in the Trump Administration.

A week before the election, Christie disappeared from public view as a Trump Surrogate. After the election, an astonished President Trump quickly replaced Christie with Vice President Mike Pence and son in law Jared Kushner as Transition Managers. Complaining about a rigged the system brought electoral vote benefits (victory), especially in the crucial rust belt states of Wisconsin, Michigan, and Pennsylvania. White middle class workers, displaced or seeing pay cuts from inflation, believe they suffer from a rigged system. Trump became their champion.

Democrats continued to fulfill their destiny as elitists, according to the script written by the billionaire populist.

Trump was unprepared to take on the duties of Chief Executive of the United States. He was six months behind in recruiting experienced managers to head up the Executive Departments. Even after the Transition Team woke up, it was not easy to recruit talent. Some executives were reluctant to join a chaotic Administration. Trump vetoed many possible nominees who had criticized him. He was angry at the State Department for resisting his call to lift sanctions on Russia.

State Fights Trump Gift to Russia.

In the first few weeks of the Trump presidency, his aides asked senior State Department officials to prepare papers to lift sanctions on Russia unilaterally, meaning without any corrective behavior by Russia. Daniel Fried, Chief Sanctions Coordinator, retired in February 2017 after forty years as Foreign Service Officer. Fried stated that State Department Officials came to him saying, *'My God, Can't you stop this?'* Tom Malinowski was Assistant Secretary of State for Human Rights. Fried and Malinowski lobbied Congress to codify the sanctions regime, and require Congress' approval to lift sanctions. On 2/7/17, Senators Ben Cardin (D-MD) and Lindsey Graham (R-SC) sponsored a sanctions bill in the Senate. Senators John McCain (R-AZ) and Graham propose a stronger sanctions bill in view of Russian interference in the 2016 election.

Exaggerating Victory.

Donald John Trump could not take 'yes' for an answer, and accept that, indeed, he was President of all the people. He could not reconcile the fact that he won the Electoral College Vote, while Hillary Clinton won the popular vote by nearly three million. Trump concluded, *without any supporting evidence*, that millions of illegal aliens in California and New York voted for Hillary Clinton. To make running in the popular vote second sting more, newspapers published aerial photos that showed the Inauguration of Barack Obama drew a larger crowd in 2009 than did the Trump Inauguration in 2017. Trump read the riot act to his staff. His victory was a landslide in his eyes, and his staff better tow the party line. Press Secretary Sean Spicer was fired up and ready to go off.

A visibly angry Spicer hastily called an emergency Saturday Press Conference and announced, *without any evidence*, that the crowd watching the Trump Inauguration was the largest ever. Period. Saturday Night Live's Melissa McCarthy saw a treasure trove in Spicer's angry loyalty to Trump's illusions of grandeur.

Trump spent a good deal of his first one hundred days in office trying to repair his wounded ego. He continually referred to his *imaginary* landslide victory. He refused to accept the fact that the 2016 election was a split decision. He alleged, *without any evidence*, that there was massive voter fraud. He appointed Vice President Pence to head up a commission to investigate the illusory voter fraud that denied him a landslide victory. Trump's obsession with his margin of victory has bought him to the point of malfeasance in office. Of the five hundred and fifty, or so, executive government positions he needed to fill through nominations in the first hundred days, Trump had nominated only a few dozen. A walk along the corridors of the Departments of State, Justice, and Defense would show a string of empty offices. There is no question about the Democrats causing delay in confirmation. There were hundreds of unfilled positions with no nominees submitted by the Trump Administration.

The Russian Connection.

A bizarre photo appeared in the New York Times on Wednesday, May 10, 2017. The photo showed President Trump greeting the two Sergeys, Lavrov and Kislyak, Foreign Minister and Ambassador to the U.S., respectively, of the Russian Federation. The meeting took place at the White House. The *Russian Foreign Ministry* supplied the photo to the Times. President Trump *barred* U.S. journalists from attending the meeting. If President Trump is innocent of any collusion with the Russians in their hack of the Clinton Campaign and interference with the 2016 U.S. presidential election, he continually does things that create doubts. Throughout the campaign, he has praised President Putin. He becomes defensive and combative whenever the subject of Russian interference in the U.S. election raised. He has been doing a slow burn over the investigations into any connection between the Trump Campaign and the Russians.

Seventeen U.S. intelligence services concluded that the Russians interfered in the U. S. presidential election in 2016. The House and Senate are investigating. The President has no control over Congress. The FBI has been investigating the Russian interference for more than one year. FBI Director James B. Comey showed no willingness to accede to Trump's desire to quash the FBI investigation of the Russian Connection. In fact, Comey submitted a budget request to Justice for an increase in funding for resources needed to expand the FBI investigation. Trump blew his stack. He met with Attorney General Jeff Sessions and Deputy Attorney General Rod Rosenstein. Trump stated that he was ready to fire Comey. He asked Sessions and Rosenstein to put their recommendation in writing. Rosenstein catalogued Comey's missteps in the investigation of Hillary Clinton's email procedures while Secretary of State.

Trump Fires FBI Chief.

Comey offended most Democrats by trashing Clinton for sloppy email procedures during her tenure as Secretary of State. Comey offended most Republicans by, at the same time, by stating that there would be no prosecution of Clinton. As a former U.S. Attorney and Acting Attorney General, Comey was accustomed to making decisions to prosecute or not. Comey was out of his lane, when, as FBI Director, he announced that there would be no prosecution of Clinton. Comey's duty was to report the facts to the Department of Justice, and allow Justice to decide on the question of prosecution. Since President Obama was still in office, the President likely did not object to Comey's announcement of no prosecution. It seems strange that a successor president could terminate an FBI Director for what was essentially a political act approved by the prior president.

Ironically, everyone knows that President Trump fired Comey on May 9, 2017, for refusing to wind down the FBI investigation into the Russian Connection to the 2016 presidential election. The pretext for the firing, of course, was Comey's missteps in the investigation of Hillary Clinton's email procedures.

The Other Elephant in the Room.

The other elephant is so immense that Republicans are not willing to tackle the problem, or even acknowledge that there is a problem. Here is one of the parameters of the size of the task. Son in law Jared Kushner is an international real estate developer with assets in the range of $600 million. Kushner works with or in association with Trump Enterprises, whose net worth may be four billion dollars, although Trump claims ten billion. Trump has golf courses and hotels from Scotland to Saudi Arabia. It is not merely a question of where Trump is doing business.

What is the source of Trump's operating and investment capital? In the past, Eric Trump suggested that money was pouring in from Russia. Eric denies stories about Russian Money. National Security Adviser Michael Flynn compromised himself because the Russians knew he lied about the content of telephone conversations he had with Ambassador Kislyak. Flynn maintained that he never discussed economic sanctions with the Russians. FBI transcripts of the conversations proved otherwise. Flynn also had problems for not complying with the Foreign Agents Registration Act ("FARA") for taking money from Russia and Turkey. Congress enacted FARA to combat propaganda of foreign powers. Congress likely had the *Big Lie* in mind when it enacted FARA.

Would FARA apply to the president of the U.S, while in office? U.S. presidents generally do not represent foreign powers. What about *The Manchurian Candidate*? Special Counsel Robert Mueller may face that question. Does a person suffering from post-hypnotic mind control have intent to violate the law? If the Russians brainwashed Donald Trump on one of his trips to Russia, who is Trump's *U.S. based Operator*? What device did the Russians employ as the Queen of Diamonds trigger?

Belated FARA Registration.

Two Trump associates registered under FARA after the fact. Lt. Gen. (Ret.) Michael Flynn, Trump's sacked National Security Adviser, registered in connection with his acceptance of $45,000 from Russia Today (RT) and $450,000 from Turkey. Former Trump Campaign Manager Paul Manafort registered to acknowledge his position as adviser to Putin puppet Viktor Yanukovych, former President of Ukraine. Flynn will also have to answer for his failure to obtain Pentagon permission to take money from Russia and Turkey.

Follow the Money.

Just as in any mystery, the riddle will solve by following the money. With the Trump Organization, there is a lot of money to follow to financially stressed projects. There is the Trump Tower in Montreal that was insolvent. Russian State Bank VEB bailed it out. VEB bought stock of the builder, who denied that Trump was his partner. As a businessperson, Donald Trump was notorious for not paying bank loans. Trump's defalcations were not a matter of thousands or tens of thousands of dollars. His defaults ranged from tens of millions to hundreds of millions. Trump so tarnished his reputation by defaults that no bank in New York would lend to him on any type of loan, secured or not. There was one New York Bank, which did keep lending to Trump, namely, Deutsche Bank. It is not evident why Deutsche Bank continued to accept Trump as a loan risk.

Just before the 2017 election, Deutsche Bank made a $285 million loan to Jared Kushner. Kushner may also have talked with Russia State Bank VEB about refinancing his company's tower at 666 Fifth Avenue. Trump Family and Organization have massive conflicts of interest that interfere with the management of the U.S. Government by Donald Trump and Jared Kushner. Even if the worldwide economic interests of Kushner and Trump and the Trump Organization were not adverse to the economic interests of the United States, the demands on the time and energy of Kushner and Trump militate against their managing the U.S. Government.

President Pence?

Rumors on the Democrats side are that the President could remove under the Twenty-fifth Amendment. The Vice President and Cabinet could aver that the President is physically or mentally unable to discharge the duties of president. This fantasy will not happen. What would happen if the Congress impeaches the President for colluding with Russian interference with the 2016 Presidential Election? Could Mike Pence succeed to the presidency if the Russia investigation topples the president? Impeachment for collusion with the Russians likely will reach the President by inculpating the Vice President first. The connecting facts will relate to the reckless actions of Lt. Gen. (Ret.) Michael Flynn, who recently registered as a Foreign Agent for Turkey in 2015-2016.

As Chair of the Trump Transition Team, Pence will scarcely be able to deny knowledge of Flynn's activities, including taking money from Russia Today. The Justice Department may have briefed Pence on dangers presented by Flynn. National Security Adviser Flynn remained in office for twenty-four days after Acting Attorney General Sally Yates informed White House Counsel Don McGahn that the Russians could blackmail Flynn for denying he discussed sanctions with Russian Ambassador Sergey Kislyak. Is it a coincidence that FBI and NSA records reportedly show that Flynn called Kislyak multiple times the same day President Obama announced sanctions against Russia?

Trump Tires &Makes Mistakes.

It is ironic that candidate Donald Trump crushed Jeb Bush's campaign with the term 'low energy', and claimed that Hillary Clinton had to take a nap after her Campaign Rallies. During the primary campaign, Trump never stayed overnight in a city where he held a rally. He always flew the Trump jet back to New York and the comfort of Fifth Avenue and Trump Tower. No one is saying whether he slept on the plane on the way home. He thought it was easy to be President, until he took the oath of office. On his first trip abroad, he complained to aides that the trip was too long and scheduled too many countries to visit. He clearly is tiring, and making more mistakes. He wants the Courts to ignore his Campaign Statements and twitter storms over banning Moslems. Courts will give a president the benefit of the doubt when it comes to interpreting a sound policy that distorts a bit viewed by an offhand campaign remark.

Trump's Campaign and statements, however, have consistently shown that he intended to ban Moslems. He cannot tell the Courts that he was only kidding. The U.S. Supreme Court agreed to take the lawsuits challenging the Moslem Ban. The Ban of visa applicants from six Moslem countries will stand, except for applicants, who have a job in the U.S., or are students in the U.S., or are relatives of U.S. residents. Refugees without any connection to the U.S. may not enter.

Trump's attempt to play Godfather to the GOP Healthcare Bill is a total failure. During the 2016 Campaign, Trump mimicked the Party Line to *'Repeal and Replace'* Obamacare, painting himself into another corner. Speaker Ryan rammed a barebones Repeal and Replace Bill through the House. Trump held a celebration in the Rose Garden. Professionals, including the AMA and AHA, denounced the Ryan Bill for taking Medicaid away from twenty three million citizens. Trump changed course, and called the Ryan Bill *"mean"*. The Senate ginned up a bill in secret that would take Medicaid away from twenty two million citizens. A Trump leaning Political Action Committee ran ads in Nevada to brow beat Senator Dean Heller into supporting the Senate Bill.

Majority Leader Mitch McConnell called Chief of Staff Reince Priebus to complain that the ad campaign against Heller was beyond stupid. Trump unleashed a twitterstorm to claim that he knew all about Healthcare. Trump came to Washington as the expert on the *Art of the Deal*. He has unmasked himself as a bull in a china shop, with his tirades against Mexicans, Mexico, Moslems, Iran, the Moslem Ban, his total ignorance of healthcare and lack of understanding of the protocols of the House of Representatives and the Senate.

We are living through an untenable time in the U.S. We cannot continue as a democratic Republic under a Leader who is a Master of the *Big Lie*. Our president's reputation for falsehoods is as notorious as is his record of loan defaults and bankruptcies. He cannot continue in power without further corrupting our democratic principles. He has attacked our news media as fake news. He has dismissed the FBI Director. There are rumors that he will dismiss Special Counsel Muller. If he dismisses Mueller, he likely will dismiss Deputy Attorney General Rod Rosenstein to block appointment of another Special Counsel. He is trying to corrupt the Justice Department. He has denigrated the U.S. Intelligence Agencies. Because of personal pique, he is starving the State Department of budget funds necessary to carry out its diplomatic mission.

Conflicts Of Interest as High Misdemeanors

Trump and Jared Kushner are not traitors because of their flirtation with Russia or for any other reason or theory. Neither is sacked Security Advisor, Lt. Gen. (Ret.) Michael Flynn. Congress could Impeach and Remove Trump from the Office of President of the United States because of massive conflicts of interest. In plain terms, Trump is too busy trying to protect his vast business interests to attend properly to the strategic interests of the Nation. Trump's

Chief Ambassador, substitute Secretary of State, confidante, counsellor on Executive Policies, and son in law, Jared Kushner, was rightly concerned about refinancing the $1.2 billion dollar mortgage note against his company's property at 666 Fifth Avenue, N.Y.

It is contrary to the interest of the Nation, however, for Kushner to take his financial problems to Russian Ambassador Sergey Kislyak, who referred Kushner to Russian Billionaire Sergey Gorkov and VEB Russia State Bank. Trump and Kushner have seen it demonstrated before their eyes how quickly foreign entanglement can compromise a U.S. Government official, such as Lt. Gen. (Ret.) Michael Flynn, and result in swift removal from office.

Russia is an implacable enemy of the United States. Russia has interfered with democratic elections in Europe and the U.S., including the U.S. 2016 Presidential election. Russia held many of the nations of Eastern Europe hostage for up to fifty years. It is an official policy of Russia to weaken and destroy the North Atlantic Treaty Organization (NATO) a mutual defense pact between the U.S., Canada, and Europe since 1949. Candidate Donald Trump saw NATO as obsolete. Russian President Vladimir Putin saw NATO as threatening to Russia's expansionist plans.

The Pecker Conspiracy.

Joe Scarborough and Mika Brzezinski cohost MSNBC's *Morning Joe* commentary. On June 28, 2017, they displayed a fake Time Magazine cover featuring Donald Trump. Some of Trump's properties hang the framed cover for viewing. Trump retaliated with a twitterstorm referring to Crazy Mika and Psycho Joe. Trump claimed they came to Trump's Mira Lago Club to join the Trump party over the holidays. Trump said no because he claims Mika was bleeding from face-lift surgery. Prominent Republicans, including Speaker Ryan and Susan Collins, denounced the Trump tweets as beneath the dignity of the office of the president. This is not the scandal, however.

The scandal is that that the President of the United States has a collaborative relationship with David Pecker, Chief Executive Officer of the *National Enquirer*, which Trump uses to slime opponents. On 6/30/17, Scarborough and Brzezinski alleged on Morning Joe that White House aides called them more than once to suggest that Joe call the President to apologize for adverse coverage during the first few months of the Trump Presidency. If Joe did not apologize, White House aides allegedly suggested that the *National Enquirer* would run a derogatory exposé on the two hosts. Joe did not apologize. The *Enquirer* ran the print story June 5, 2017. Jared Kushner reportedly was one of the White House aides who called Joe Scarborough.

If true, the story would demonstrate that President Trump has not changed since he took office, that he is still self-absorbed in ego salving vendettas, and that he is distracted from the performance of his duties to the Nation. The *National Enquirer* denies that it coordinated publication of the story with the White House.

Chapter 11

Special Counsel's Mission.

Special Counsel Robert Mueller has a broad mandate (1) to investigate the extent of Russian interference in the U.S. presidential election of 2016, (2) to determine whether the Trump Campaign colluded with the Russians, and (3) to prosecute violations of U.S. law, if any, with respect to the Russian interference and collusion, if any, by the Trump Campaign. The task is simple. Mueller must lay out a roadmap that shows what the Russians and any U.S. collaborators did in 2015 and 2016 to disrupt the U.S. election. Completing the roadmap, however, requires slogging through reports of espionage and conducting interviews of dozens of individuals in an effort to sort out facts from fiction and rumors.

Seventeen U.S. intelligence Agencies have concluded that the Russians interfered. The principal repositories of intelligence on espionage and counterespionage are the CIA and the FBI. Mueller will use available intelligence reports for a start. He will employ staff from personnel of the FBI and the Justice Department. He will develop leads from the available intelligence. His staff will explore those leads. His staff will interview key players from the Trump Campaign, as well as state election officials. Russia, of course, will not cooperate.

Ghosts from the Past.

If Peter W. Smith is a ghost, he is a newly minted one having died in May 2017. He did have a past, however, in Clinton bashing. Smith, a banker from Chicago, has been active in GOP Opposition Research for years. Smith dug up some of the dirt on Bill Clinton, then Governor of Arkansas, in the Troopergate Scandal in the 1990s. According to Shane Harris, who interviewed Smith for the Wall Street Journal, Smith convened a meeting after Labor Day in September 2016 to look for persons who might be able to produce Hillary Clinton emails. The story could dismiss as fantasy. In view of Smith's past in GOP Opposition Research, however, and the documented Russian interference in 2016, the Office of Special Counsel should look into it.

The story implied that Smith was looking for Hillary emails from various groups, including the Russians to give the emails to Lt. Gen. (Ret.) Michael Flynn. The story does not add up because there is no explanation for Smith "confessing" a few months before he passed on. Smith may have died an ardent GOP partisan. If so, the interview with WSJ's Shane Harris may have been a time bomb designed to blow up in the Democrats' faces when it proved illusory.

President Teddy Roosevelt used the Bully Pulpit of the Presidency to try to influence events and individuals. President Trump unleashes tweets to threaten and intimidate folks he fears. His latest nemesis is FBI Director James B. Comey, whom Trump fired summarily on May 9, 2017. Trump feared that Comey would leak to the press or testify to Congress with derogatory but truthful information that would disclose embarrassing facts. *Trumped tweeted that Comey better be sure that Trump did not record the conversation between them at a private White House dinner.* In his letter removing Comey from office, and released through public media, Trump thanked Comey for allegedly assuring Trump on three separate occasions that the FBI was not investigating Trump.

The former virtual reality television star desperately tried to create his own virtual reality by tweeting what he wishes the state of facts were. Trump fired Comey precisely because Comey would not give Trump any assurances about winding down the FBI investigation into the possible Connection between his Campaign and Russian Interference in the 2016 Presidential election.

According to former Deputy CIA Director Mike Morrell, there are five Power Centers in the White House.

> Nationalists led by Stephen Bannon and Stephen Miller;
> Globalists led by National Security Adviser Gen. (Ret.) H.L. McMaster, Gen (Ret.) Mattis at Defense, and Gen. (Ret.) John Kelly at Homeland Security;
> Protective Family Members led by son in law Jared Kushner and daughter Ivanka Kushner;
> Donald John Trump, the 45th President of the United States; and
> Base Supporters

In reality, there is one power center in the White House. That is Donald Trump. He may listen to Stephen Bannon and Stephen Miller, and even tune in to Alex Jones' Info Wars on occasion. At the end of the day, Bannon works for Trump. Jared Kushner and Ivanka have a moderating influence on Trump. There is a Unitary Executive. Trump wields the Executive Power. That is the reason he was furious with Attorney General Sessions for recusing himself from decisions relating to the Russian Investigation. Trump wanted to control the Russian Investigation, more than he did anything else.

Nationalists do not like the Environmental Protection Agency, United Nations, NATO, the Paris Accords on Climate Change, or Cold War treaties that tie the U.S. to defense of Europe and Japan. Nationalists want to see more jobs for coalminers in West Virginia and Pennsylvania and for American workers in general, a wall constructed on the border with Mexico, a ban on Moslems entering the U.S. from six predominately Moslem Countries (that had no connection with the 9/11/01 attack on America), and more deportation of illegal aliens. Globalists want the U.S. to continue to lead the world on matters of international cooperation, free trade, a strong NATO, and continued cooperation and trade with Europe and Japan. U.S. foreign and domestic policy gyrates from one extreme to the other as President Trump vacillates between the Nationalists and the Globalist.

Russia, of course is delighted with Trump's assault on Germany, Europe, and NATO. If Ukraine was considering joining NATO, what is the mindset of Estonia, Latvia, and Lithuania, Baltic Republics formerly under control of the Soviet Union? Trump visited Europe in May 2017 and notably did not reaffirm U.S. support of Article 5 of NATO, which states that an attack on one NATO Member is an attack on all Members. Russia had no fear of taking back Crimea by force of arms and invading eastern Ukraine in 2014. Since Trump shows favor toward Russia and indifference or hostility toward NATO, should President Putin of Russia make plans to re-take the Baltic States?

Security Clearance Landmines.

Top officials of every Administration must complete questionnaires to qualify for security clearance necessary for their position. One question, about contacts with Russians, created memory problems for Trump's closest confidants. Attorney General Jeff Sessions forgot that he met twice with Russian Ambassador Sergey Kislyak. At his confirmation hearing, Sessions denied contact with Russia. He made the same mistake on his Security Questionnaire. Jared Kushner forgot that he met with Russians multiple times. Special Counsel Mueller has a roadmap for the Russia Investigation. On advice of counsel, Jared Kushner revised his Security Questionnaire three times. Among other things, Kushner disclosed a meeting on June 9, 2016, with a Russian Lawyer connected to the Kremlin. Donald Trump, Jr., and Paul Manafort also attended.

This revelation by Kushner forced a correction by Donald Trump, Jr., who had denied meeting with Russians during the 2015 2106 Campaign. Trump's son issued two conflicting statements. On Saturday, July 8, 2017, he said he accompanied Kushner and Manafort to a meeting where a Russian attorney started speaking about adoption of Russian children. On Sunday, July 9, he said the three top Trump Campaign officials attended the meeting for the announced purpose of obtaining information that would help the Trump Campaign. The Russian Lawyer hinted that Russians were contributing to the Hillary Campaign. When the Lawyer's statements remained vague and without substantiation, Team Trump ended the meeting.

Rob Goldstone, a music publicist, was the intermediary between the Trump Campaign and the Russian Lawyer, Natalia Veselnitskaya. To preempt the New York Times expected publication, Donald Trump Jr. released the text of email from Rob Goldstone, promising incriminating information on Hillary Clinton from the Russian State Prosecutor's office. Goldstone represents Emin Agaralov, an Azerbaijani pop singer and son of wealthy developer, Aras Agaralov, who arranged for Trump to bring the 2013 Miss Universe Contest to his Crocus City Hall in Moscow. In the email chain to Donald, Jr., Goldstone promised incriminating information on Clinton. Donald, Jr. said, *'I love it'*. Don, Jr., claims the meeting on June 9 did not produce *dirt* on Hillary.

It is a violation of U.S. Campaign Law to accept anything of value from a foreign power with respect to a political campaign. Title 2 United States Code §441e. *'It shall be unlawful for a foreign national ...to make any contribution of money or other thing of value ... in connection with an election....'*

The President and Melania are off to Paris without Jared Kushner on 7/12/17 for a Bastille Day Celebration with President of France, Emmanuel Macron. Donald Trump, Jr., and Paul Manafort are not employees of the U.S. Government. Jared Kushner, however, has a top-secret security clearance as an aide to the President. To obtain the security clearance, Kushner had to complete Form SF86, the security questionnaire. Team Trump uniformly denied any meeting with the Russians for one year. Kushner revised his Form SF86 at least twice to disclose meetings with the Russians. The President may consider resignation to protect his family and himself. First, Vice President Mike Pence should resign to start with a clean slate.

Eventually, someone at the top will talk, whether Lt. Gen. (Ret.) Michael Flynn or Jared Kushner. There is urgency to complete the investigation. The United States has jeopardy, whether from a President who is *The Manchurian Candidate*, or from a blackmail victim in the White House who is subject to control by Russia.

Trump has lost the confidence of the majority of Americans. He fooled the People with the Big Lie, the *Little Lie*, reality distortion, propaganda, cover-up of Team Trump's collusion with the Russians, and misdirection. He cannot hold a press conference because he cannot face the questions about the Russia investigation. He makes a mockery of White House briefings by banning audio, video, or both. He can control the news that comes out of the White House, but no one believes Team Trump on denials of the Russian connection. Trump led Team Trump in lies and a massive cover up for over a year.

Trump still talks of a witch-hunt, fake news, and anonymous sources. The source of the email chain—that showed the meeting with Natalia Veselnitskaya to obtain criminal evidence against Hillary Clinton from the Russia State prosecutor—was Donald Trump, Jr.

Russia wants the U.S. isolated. Trump walked away from the Paris Climate Accord. Trump wants America First on trade matters. Germany's Angela Merkel decided that Trump is unreliable, and that Europe can no longer look to the U.S. for leadership. Russia wants NATO weakened. Trump stated that NATO is obsolete. Trump failed as a world leader at the 2017 G20 meeting in Hamburg. He did not deal forcefully with Russian interference in the 2016 election. Trump excluded the media and his own National Security Adviser from the side meeting with Vladimir Putin. Trump suggested that Russia and the U.S. should form an impenetrable unit to combat computer hacking. Putin continues to play Team Trump as fools and amateurs.

One question that calls out for answer is who will be the second and third members of the Administration to resign after Lt. Gen. (Ret.) Michael Flynn? The President's lawyers do not want Jared Kushner talking with their client about Russian interference. Kushner may find he is odd man out, despite marriage with Ivanka Trump. Pointedly, Kushner and Ivanka did not accompany Trump to Paris on 7/12/17. Neither did Stephen Bannon because of his theory that NATO is obsolete. Rex Tillerson is restless. As former head of Exxon Mobil, he cannot abide with taking instructions from young White House Staffers. If Kushner leaves, Tillerson may have a portfolio at the State Department.

GOP Brand Tarnished.

Republicans control the House, Senate, and White House. They are unable to accomplish anything, however. Two items consume all time and energy. First, the constant drip of revelations of collusion by Team Trump with the Russians to interfere with the 2016 presidential election, and a cover-up that included firing the Director of the FBI to stop the investigation. Second, the fixation of the GOP to drive a stake through the heart of Obamacare by outright repeal. By declaring Obamacare dead, the President and GOP legislators encourage insurers to restrict area coverage and to increase premiums for areas covered. Distortions in the health insurance market ultimately will demonstrate the benefits of single payer coverage.

Speaker Paul Ryan, second in line of succession to the presidency, is not willing to jump off the Trump Train until a crash is evident. By that time, it will be too late. Because of Russian interference in the 2016 election, the Senate passed an increased sanctions bill against Russia by a vote of 97 to 2. Whether as an unwitting asset of Russia, or an egotist, President Trump lobbied Speaker Ryan to delay or gut the Senate Bill. If Ryan fails to protect America from at-tack on its democratic principles by the criminal enterprise that controls Russia, the GOP will lose control of the House and Senate.

'I continue to oppose the process House republicans included in the bill that would only al-low the Speaker of the House to force consideration of whether to allow the Administration to waive sanctions.' House Democratic Whip Steny Hoyer (MD), July 11, 2017.

GOP hypocrisy is hard to conceal. Opposition to Obamacare since 2009 is a charade de-signed to confuse the American People. Republicans do not want a federal healthcare bill. It is not a question of fine-tuning the *Affordable Care Act* (ACA). GOP lawmakers want to please the one percent of the wealthiest constituents, who make most of the political contributions. The wealthy can afford to pay for the best medical care outside the ACA. The one percent do not want a federal healthcare bill.

Senate Majority Leader Mitch McConnell is playing a bait and switch game with Senate Re-publicans. He is modifying the GOP Bill to garner fifty votes on Motion to Proceed. After agreement to proceed carries, the bill will morph back to a massive tax cut for the wealthy, coupled with a savage cut to Medicaid. GOP Judas Goats will lull the People to sleep with promises of block grants to the states, which, in turn will make cuts in Medicaid. In the mean-time, President Trump presides over the *Big Lie* in the White House bubble, while waiting, pen in hand, to sign the death warrant for Obamacare.

Chapter 12

Post-Hypnotic Mind Control.

Brainwashing.

New World Encyclopedia defines *'brainwashing'* as 'the systematic application of coercive techniques to change beliefs or behavior of people usually for political or religious purposes'. The Chinese use the same metaphor, in pinyin transliteration, 'xi Nao' ('to wash the brain') a play on the religious exhortation 'xi Xin' (to wash the heart).The Pentagon referred to 'brainwashing' in the 1950s as the explanation for a number of captured military of U. S and other United Nations countries adopting communist ideas in the Korean War. The brass happily reported that most POWs, upon release, abandoned ideas of Marx and Lenin. It should come as no surprise that POWs will at least pretend to agree with their jailers to avoid starvation and infliction of physical and psychological pain.

"Brainwashing is said to reduce its subject's ability to think critically or independently." Wikipedia, Brainwashing, citing Encyclopaedic Dictionary of Religion, Vol. 2, Gyan Publishing House, 2005. Despite reports of brainwashing by Chinese in the Korean War, the U.S. Army failed to document even one case where the Chinese succeeded in turning a U.N. prisoner. *Communist Interrogation, Indoctrination, and Exploitation of Prisoners of War* 1956, p. 51.

Mind Control.

'Is Total Mind Control Possible?' In *Psychology Today*, web posted 9/24/15, John Ryder, Ph.D., says, *'No'. 'You cannot be programmed to become a killer without your knowledge. Hypnosis can be persuasive, but does not give the hypnotist control over your mind, morality, or judgment.'* Hypnotism, however, can confuse morality and judgment by suggesting that a subject's loved ones will be at risk, or, perhaps, the security of the Nation will be imperiled, if the subject does not perform the instructed task.

On May 13, 2017, President Trump gave the commencement address at Liberty University, Lynchburg, Virginia, a conservative college founded by the late Jerry Falwell and managed by his son. Trump needed to shore up his conservative credentials. Senator John McCain made his pilgrimage to Lynchburg when he ran for President. McCain was a maverick, and not a true conservative. Trump urged the Liberty graduates to be outsiders. Trump claimed that no one made important contributions except outsiders. Everything Trump does or says revolves around his ravenous ego. His message at Liberty was that he is the ultimate outsider. Emulate the Donald and be a great person. There is more to the message, however. Trump lays groundwork for ego repair far ahead of events.

A year before he won the 2016 election, he claimed the system is rigged, thereby cushioning the embarrassment of an anticipated loss to Hillary Clinton. Trump urged Liberty graduates to keep on doing what they were doing, even when criticized. The Liberty Address was Trump's *Apologia Pro Vita Sua.*

Falwell was cofounder of the Moral Majority in 1979. Traditional Baptist principles suggested a separation of religion from politics. Falwell, the leader of the country's largest Baptist congregation, saw the nation falling away from the lifestyle Falwell saw as moral. Falwell became a force in conservative, Republican politics, supporting Ronald Reagan for President in 1980. After Reagan's presidency, Falwell dissolved the organization in 1989. Jerry Falwell, Jr, took over Liberty University after his father's passing. Politicians like Lindsey Graham, John McCain and Donald Trump, who seek support of the religious right, still make their pilgrimages to Liberty University.

As part of a long-range strategic plan to run as Republican candidate, Trump assumed the leadership of the *Birther Movement* in 2011. Trump feared that GOP Party leaders would not accept him as the Republican candidate for President. Trump knew that most Republicans had an irrational loathing for the Nation's first African American President. Attacking President Obama as illegitimate would fire up the GOP Base. Trump knew Barack Obama was born in the United States. The truth did not matter to Trump. What mattered was the fan club that Trump would draw to salve his flagging ego and boost his political capital. Trump now fears he may not last four years as President.

The Courts stopped his outright Moslem Travel Ban. There is a firestorm of criticism over his clumsy and suspicious firing of FBI Director James B. Comey. At the time his termination became public, Comey was speaking from the podium to FBI employees in Los Angeles. Comey thought the news flash was a prank.

Seventeen U.S. intelligence services determined that Russia interfered with the U.S. 2016 election. The FBI, the House, and the Senate are also investigating the Russian connection to the Trump Campaign. Paul Manafort managed the Trump Campaign. Until 2014, Manafort was adviser to Viktor Yanukovych, Putin's puppet in the Ukraine. General Michael Flynn, Trump's Security Adviser, received remuneration from Russia and from Turkey without Defense Department approval. Flynn lied about telephone conversations he had with Russian Ambassador Sergey Kislyak. Sally Yates, Acting Attorney General, informed White House Counsel that the Russians could blackmail Flynn over his lies. Trump fired Flynn a few weeks later. Carter Page, a Trump advisor on foreign policy made numerous trips to Russia. Trump dissociated from Page before Inauguration.

Shake-Up of White House Staff?

After a stormy 110 + days in office, rumors swirled about an expected shake-up of White House Staff. Trump blames his staff for his low poll ratings. Early on, Trump was dissatisfied with the performance of Press Secretary Sean Spicer. He chided Spicer on not looking professional enough. Spicer appeared at the next Press Conference in a different suit. The Press Conference routine, however, remained the same. Reporters continued to ask questions that Spicer could not address, deflect, or explain away. Melissa McCarthy's parody of Spicer on *Saturday Night Live* may have been the last straw. Trump is convinced that bad press is favorable because of the attention received. Ridicule is not helpful.

Spicer contributed to his predicament by relying on dangerous comparisons. In trying to show Bashar al Assad, Syrian Dictator, as worse than Hitler was, Spicer floated the lie that at least Hitler never killed anyone with gas. Spicer apologized for misstating history, and admitted that he let the President down. The problem does not lie with Sean Spicer or the Chief of Staff Reince Priebus. Donald Trump has no core convictions. Spicer has trouble defending Trump's actions because Trump's actions frequently are indefensible. If Trump were justified in firing FBI Chief Comey over handling of the investigation of Hillary Clinton's email procedures, that firing should have happened in February 2017, not in May.

Trump was not concerned about the FBI's Investigation of Clinton, who now is no threat to the White House. Trump worried about the FBI's investigation of the Russian Connection with the Trump Campaign. When Comey did not give assurances to button things up, Trump fired him.

Heat from Paris to Pittsburgh.

On June 1, 2017, Trump announced his decision to take the U.S. out of the *Paris Climate Accords*, thereby sabotaging world efforts to reduce carbon dioxide emissions that scientists believe contribute to global warming and extreme weather conditions. Steve Bannon, other insiders, and White House Staff applauded. The rest of the world is in shock. Only Syria and Nicaragua refused to sign on. As the world's largest emitter of carbon dioxide, the U.S. should remain a leader in finding a solution. Trump curiously countered that he represented the people of Pittsburgh, not the people of Paris, apparently not realizing that Pittsburgh exited steel making seventy years ago. The Mayor of Pittsburgh promptly denounced Trump's pulling the U.S. out. France, Germany, and Italy jointly regretted Trump's decision.

Jeff Immelt, at the time CEO of General Electric, announced that U.S. industry would have to lead instead of government. A dozen other Fortune Five Hundred companies rejected Trump's move. In an unrelated move, GE replaced Immelt as CEO with John Flannery to optimize the company's business lines.

The Sierra Club offered congratulations to *President Bannon*, who continually leads Trump down the *Rabbit Hole to Blunder Land*. The United Kingdom withdrew from the European Union through its Brexit Vote in 2016. Trump has exhibited particular indifference to Germany and its Chancellor, Angela Merkel, for the past year, leading Merkel to remark that Europeans can no longer depend on others for security. Trump's jettisoning of the Paris Climate Accords is the last straw. China is marching into the vacuum in Europe created by the Trump Bannon strategy. Somewhere in the U.S., there must be an Archie Bunker clone, who is ecstatic. He would not be in Pittsburgh, however. Possibly, Gary, Indiana. One-reason Trump dislikes Germany is that the Germans run a trade surplus with the U.S. and most of the world. Leaving the Paris Climate Accord, however, will not produce jobs in the U.S.

Why Would V. Putin Want Trump In A Trance?

Trump is the ideal candidate for post hypnotic mind control. Trump is untouchable. No one can get to Trump other than if there is a *U.S. operator* for post-hypnotic suggestion. Trump has Secret Service protection 24/7 at the White House, at Mira Lago, at Camp David, and everywhere the President travels at home and abroad. If the President is an involuntary asset of Russia, the United States will keep Putin's asset in a protective bubble, isolated from external forces. Trump's psychological profile is perfect for mind control. He has a strong ego. He is competitive. He makes countercultural and controversial statements. He has a record of seeking support from xenophobic and socially antagonistic groups. In the context of where he has been on his pet issues and what he has said, there is little more he can say or do that would make him appear more abnormal or dangerous.

He is a master propagandist and a master publicist. Even the CIA and FBI cannot be sure if the President's propaganda is coming from Trump, Bannon, and Miller, or from V. Putin and the FSB. It is ironic that everything Trump does helps Russia directly or indirectly. Because FBI Director James B. Comey refused to back off the investigation of Lt. Gen. (Ret.) Michael Flynn and Russian interference in the 2016 presidential election, the President fired Comey. Deputy Attorney General Rod Rosenstein appointed former FBI Director Robert Mueller Special Counsel to head the Russian investigation. Former Speaker Newt Gingrich praised the appointment of Mueller. A friend of the President announced that the President was considering firing Mueller. The White House denied the report. Someone in the White House got to Newt Gingrich.

Newt suddenly saw Mueller's appointment as a Democratic plot, and noted that Comey, as Acting Attorney General for Bush, appointed Richard Fitzgerald to investigate the outing of Valerie Plame as a CIA Agent. Trump is concerned that Mueller and Comey are good friends, and that Mueller is hiring attorneys who contributed to the campaigns of Hillary Clinton and Barack Obama. No matter what Trump says or does, it will fit his profile. The Nation will not be alert to take action until it is too late to act. The CIA and the FBI suffer institutional paralysis caused by doubt, fear, suspicion, and internal conflict. The Justice Department is paralyzed. The Attorney General recused himself from the Russian investigation. Special Counsel Mueller faces accusations of favoritism toward Comey, Obama, and Clinton. Putin is delighted.

The Republican Congress is paralyzed by its fixation on driving a stake through the heart of Obamacare, in contrast to the Peoples' insistence that Obamacare be continued and expanded. Nothing will progress in Washington, because the President of the United States is the Chief Executive of the CIA, the FBI, and the Justice Department, and the President does not want the Russian investigation to go forward. Homeland Security cannot do its job because of security. Russian cyber hackers broke into the computers of around twenty-one states. Elections in the United States are under state control. When state Secretaries of State requested information from Homeland Security about Russian interference in the 2016 election, Homeland Security refused to cooperate because state Secretaries of State do not have appropriate Secret Clearances.

The only viable solution to the institutional paralysis in Washington is to impeach the President. It is doubtful that the CIA, FBI, Justice Department, Special Counsel Muller or Congress can show that the President is *The Manchurian Candidate*. There are signs, however, and events that cannot dismiss as mere coincidences. Trump said on many occasions that. *'It would be nice if we could get along with Russia'*. The President criticized other NATO countries. Trump replaced his Campaign Manager with Paul Manafort, adviser to Viktor Yanukovych, Putin's man in charge of Ukraine. Trump consultant Cater Page made several trips to Moscow. Lt. Gen (Ret.) Michael Flynn took $45,000 from Russia Today (RT), a propaganda arm of Putin. Who picked Rex Tillerson to be Secretary of State?

V. Putin thought Tillerson was an excellent choice. As Head of Exxon Mobil, Tillerson oversaw the contract between Exxon Mobil and Russia for development of Russia's oil reserves. Putin awarded Tillerson the *Order of Friendship*, formerly known as the *Order of Lenin,* for good and faithful service. Tillerson is a loyal American, who would likely be Putin's choice for Secretary of State.

We do not know who is Trump's *U.S. operator*, or what the *Queen of Diamonds* might be. The plan, however, is clear. President Obama placed sanctions on Russia, stopping the Russian contracts with Exxon Mobil, because of Putin's aggression against Ukraine. President Trump wanted to lift the sanctions on Russia as his first order of business. Tillerson would bring American technology to Russian oil fields. In January 2017, the President requested the State Department to prepare to lift the sanctions against Russia. State refused the request, and complained to Congress. The President retaliated by cutting State's budget by 25%, and by delaying nominations for Under Secretaries and other top officials at State. .*What we are witnessing before our eyes is that a hostile power has taken control of the government of the United States.*

What if Donald Trump is the *U.S. Operator* for the 35% of Americans who are under control of his twitter feed? What if Trump's Base collectively are *The Manchurian Candidate* subject to post-hypnotic mind control? More frightening is that 80% of Republicans think Trump is swell.

End Notes

<u>Foreword</u>.

'Kompromat'. Dmitri Peskov, Putin's Public Relations Manager, claims that, *"The Kremlin does not collect compromising materials".* Putin owes his rise to power to *'Kompromat'.* In 1999, Russia's State Prosecutor General, Yury Skuratov, threatened to prosecute corruption in the Kremlin. President Boris Yeltsin, chief beneficiary of that corruption, was shocked. Russia State RTR Television aired a video of Skuratov naked in bed with two women. The prosecutor had to resign. Yeltsin was so impressed with the FSB's checkmate of the prosecutor, that he bequeathed Russia to the Intelligence Officer who staged the video. That man was Vladimir Putin, Head of FSB. NPR, *All Things Considered*, Jan 11, 2017. Cf. BBC, 19 Mar 1999, *'Crisis brews over sex video'*, with no mention of Putin as the producer of the staged *Kompromat*.

Putin granted Yeltsin immunity. BBC 5 Jan 2000, *Putin faces whiff of corruption*. CBS, Sixty Minutes, *Yeltsin: Russian Democracy Firm*, Oct 06, 2000, Alberto Moya.

78

<u>Chapter 1</u>. *Stunning Surprise for Hillary Clinton on November 8, 2016.*

Russian Interference. Seventeen U.S. intelligence agencies conclude that the Russians interfered in the U.S. 2016 presidential election. President Trump questions whether the U.S. has seventeen intelligence agencies, and suggests that wat he considers slander comes from CIA and FBI. Trump resolved FBI by firing Director Comey. He smeared CIA by noting finding of WMD in Iraq in 2003. Office of the Director of National Intelligence (ODNI) assessed in January 2017 that Russian President Vladimir Putin preferred Donald Trump, and ordered a campaign to harm Hillary Clinton's campaign and undermine public faith in the U.S. democratic process. Wikipedia, *Russian Interference in the 2006 election*, notes 1-272, citing hundreds of sources.

Vladimir Putin does not deny Russian hacking into U.S. computers. He claims it is the work of *'Russian patriots'*, the same dangerous sham for taking over eastern Ukraine. According to Putin, these events did not happen *'on the state level'*. While President Trump is wasting time on recounting the 2016 popular vote, Putin is reconstituting the Soviet Union. Trump is too weak or too distracted to confront Putin's aggression. The Nation is imperiled by Trump's failure to discharge the duties of the office of president of the United States.

The Comey Firing. It is a fiction floated by President Trump that he fired FBI Chief James B. Comey on May 9, 2017, for missteps in handling the email investigation of Hillary Clinton. As reported by the New York Times, at the May 10, 2017, meeting with Sergey Lavrov and Sergey Kislyak, Russia's Foreign Minister and Ambassador, respectively, Trump referred to Comey as a *"Nut Job"*. Trump also remarked that he felt relieved from the pressure of the FBI Russian investigation after removing Comey. The initial pretext for firing Comey was that Deputy Attorney General Rod Rosenstein wrote a memo dated May 9, 2017, recommending firing for cause. Rosenstein, however, concluded from his meeting with Trump, that Trump already decided to remove Comey before Rosenstein wrote his memo. Rosenstein testimony to Congress 5/18/17.

Washington Post Blog, Election 2016, *An oral history of 2016*, presents views on what happened. Kellyanne Conway went to the heart of Hillary Clinton's penchant for safety. *"I just never have seen her as somebody who takes risks"*, pointing out that risk takers were Trump, Obama, and Bill Clinton. Robby Mook, *"I definitely remember we had a lot of angst around, like, how do we handle Trump.* Jennifer Palmieri, *"Our big concern was that he might morph into somebody else"*. Joel Benenson, *"His notion that he is a great businessman is total [bull] be-*

cause he is really a flop over and over again. But you could not convince people of that because they know he is wealthy. He is flying around in a plane with his name on it."

The problem the Democrats had was that Trump's appeal was visceral, not rational. Trump's Base does not concede to logical argument. Campaigning against Trump is akin to starting a fight in a bar.

Chapter 2, A Stormy Presidency, a *White House in Chaos*

White House in Chaos. Washington Post, January 31, 2017, *Donald Trump's White House is in chaos. And He loves it,* by Chris Cillizza. Six months later, the President loved it a lot less. The gyrations in the White House Press Conferences show dissatisfaction of the President, if not rage, exercising total control over news releases, complete with banning recordings by audio or video, or both. Dueling leaks are coming from the Bannon Miller wing and the Jared Kushner Wing. of the White House. The Executive Branch cannot oppose Russia because of internecine power struggles.

"He can't get Congress to send a healthcare bill for him to sign. His own family is causing public relations (and possibly legal) problems. He was something of an outsider the recent G20 meeting in Germany", etc. Susan Milligan, US News, July 14, 2017.

After dismissing FBI Director Comey, Trump brought to the White House Sergey Lavrov, Russia Foreign Minister, and Sergey Kislyak, Russia Ambassador, but would not allow U.S. media to attend. Russia supplied the photos to the New York Times. *Trump's handling of classified info brings new chaos to White House*, Politico May 15, 2017, by J. Dawsey, E. Johnson, and J. Meyer. "It never stops. Basically, chaos at all times", according to one White House official.

The Big Lie. This was a propaganda technique, *Die Grosse Lüge*, developed by der Führer and adopted by Propaganda Minister Josef Goebbels. The psychological profile of proponents of the *Big Lie* shows readiness to keep the public hot about the issue, never admit you made a mistake, never admit there is any good in the target, never allow an explanation that would exculpate the target, never accept blame, and concentrate on one target at a time and blame that target for everything. Office of Strategic Services (OSS) profile of der Führer, <u>Hitler as his Associates Know Him</u>, p. 51. It is important to tell a Big Lie, rather than a little one. The bigger the lie, the more people will believe it. By repeating the lie, more people will believe it. *Id.*

Mitch McConnell's flirtation with dictatorship. Senate Majority Leader McConnell, emboldened by GOP control of the White House and both Houses of Congress, suspended regular order to cobble together a secret Senate Bill to Repeal and Replace the *Affordable Care Act* (ACA). McConnell did not send the bill to the Finance Committee, where he feared it might die. He tasked his aides to draft the bill in secret, without any input from stakeholders, such as the AMA, AHA, big Pharma, or the insurance industry. McConnell excluded forty-eight Senators because they are Democrats as well as most Senators who are Republicans.

Susan Collins (R-ME) opposed the Bill because of step cuts to Medicaid. Rand Paul (R-KY) opposed because he viewed the Bill as Obamacare light. There was a panic when John McCain went to the hospital for surgery. McConnell put the Bill on hold until McCain returned. Then two more Senators announced opposition. On July 18, 2017, McConnell abandoned dictatorship to return to regular order. The House repealed ACA upwards of sixty times. In seven years, Republicans never put forward a unified Republican Plan for Healthcare. McConnell will take up the last House Bill to seek compromise. McConnell will allow Democrats to join.

Chapter 3- A Cabinet of Generals, Billionaires, and Two Women.

Trump's authoritarian nature leans toward putting generals in charge. As a respecter of money, Trump is impressed with billionaires.

Chapter 4 - *Twitter Storm: What Trump's Tweets Mean.*

Conventional wisdom is that Trump's advisers want him to stop sending out tweets. Trump, however, uses Twitter to condition, control, and fire up his Base, which can amount to 36% of the electorate, or 80% of Republican voters.

"One of the most reliable patterns of Donald Trump's presidency may be his ability to undercut his own aides—even mere hours after they attempted to defend him." CNN Politics, June 6, 2017, by Dan Merica. Sarah Huckabee Sanders said, *"I don't think the President cares what you call it."* Trump later tweeted, *"People can call it whatever they want, but I am calling it what we need and what it is, a TRAVEL BAN"*.

The truth is that the Nation will survive without a Moslem Travel Ban. Trump, Stephen Bannon and Stephen Miller know the Moslem Travel Ban will fire up the Base. The issue is strictly political. It has nothing to do with National Security.

The reason Trump cannot give up sending Tweets is that he uses Twitter for propaganda purposes to brainwash and condition the Base whom Rush Limbaugh call "dittoheads".

Chapter 5 - President Trump Forced to Pivot Toward Reality.

President Trump makes a small pivot to some sort of orthodoxy each time he reads a speech from the teleprompter. He usually reverts to impromptu remarks by force of habit. Trump knows his base admires spontaneity, which is dangerous in foreign relations. Two cartoons illustrate the risk Trump takes with Putin. Trump is thinking in one cartoon, *"I think Putin gets me."* Putin is thinking, *"I got him"*. In the other cartoon, Putin offers to help Trump with cybersecurity, and asks, 'What is your password?"

Chapter 6 - Putin Bromance, Russian Money, or Trump Compromised?

Each day, Trump appears more compromised. On January 26, 2017, Acting Attorney General Sally Yates informed White House Counsel Don McGahn that Flynn's statements on not discussing sanctions with the Russians were not true, and that Flynn was subject to blackmail by Russia. Trump had to dismiss Flynn 24 days later. Trump felt that he had to dismiss FBI Director Comey because of the pressure of the Russia investigation. Deputy Attorney General Rod Rosenstein appointed Robert Mueller Special Counsel to take over the Russia investigation independent of political interference. Team Trump denied any collusion with the Russians for more than a year.

The story of the meeting with the Russian attorney by Don, Jr., Jared Kushner, and Paul Manafort dribbled out during the second week of July 2017, and the story only grew more incriminating as Don, Jr., gave it up bit by bit in a transparent forced retreat.

Chapter 7 - Facts Are Stubborn Things That Do Not Go Away.

Facts are stubborn things, etc. John Adams, *Argument in Defense of the [British] Soldiers in the Boston Massacre Trials*, December 1770. As an impresario of a virtual reality television program, *the Apprentice*, the President invents his own facts.

Chapter 8 - Trump Denies Russian Computer Hacking.

To maintain his position of uncertainty of Russian computer hacking of the DNC and John Podesta, Trump had to attack the CIA, fire the FBI Director, and deny that seventeen US Intelligence Agencies agreed that Russia was culpable.

Chapter 9 - Little Marco, Lyin' Ted, and Crooked Hillary.

The 2016 Campaign may have hit a new low for blatant personal insult. Republicans mounted a propaganda attack against Hillary Clinton as soon as she stepped down as Secretary of State. *The Select Committee Investigation on the attack on the U.S. Mission at Benghazi, Libya,* had one purpose, to bring down Hillary's poll numbers. When Majority leader Kevin McCarthy made a speech admitting it, he lost his chance to be Speaker.

The Clintons and their advisers brought about the email fiasco. The Inspector General of the State Department was at fault for not forcing use of State Department equipment for State Department Communications.

Chapter 10 - Impeachment Remedy For Dereliction of Duty.

It matters whether Team Trump colluded with the Russians. Impeachment, however, is necessary, even without collusion, because Team Trump is entirely consumed with their own personal and business agendas. The U.S. needs a Chief Executive who can put the Nation's business ahead of his ego.

Chapter 11 - Special Counsel Robert Mueller's Mission.

"On May 17, 2017, Deputy Attorney General Rod J. Rosenstein appointed former FBI Director Robert S. Mueller III Special Counsel to oversee the previously-confirmed FBI investigation of Russian government officials to influence the 2016 presidential election and related matters."

"in my capacity as Acting Attorney General, I determined that it is in the public interest for me to exercise my authority and appoint a Special Counsel to assume responsibility for this matter." U.S Department of Justice, Office of Public Affairs, May 17, 2017.

Rosenstein acted pursuant to 28 U.S.C §§ 509, 510, and 515. *"If the Special Counsel believes it is necessary and appropriate, the Special Counsel is authorized to prosecute federal crimes arising from the investigation of these matters."* Special Counsel is empowered to combine investigative power of the FBI with the prosecutorial discretion of a United States Attorney. Special Counsel Mueller will not have to submit his findings to the Department of Justice for their decision on prosecution, as FBI Director Comey would have to do. By deciding to dismiss FBI Director Comey, Trump and Jared Kushner have lept from the frying pan into the fire.

Chapter 12 - Post-Hypnotic Mind Control

Hypnosis changes the state of the subject's mind by inducing a trance like sleep where the hypnotist is able to plant suggestions. Wikipedia, *Hypnotism*, and references.

Appendix 1

Some Of The Russian Money In Trump Properties

In general, follow the money.

From Russia to Florida.

According to Reuters, 63 private Russian individuals invested USD $98 million in Trump Florida properties. Reuters.com, 3/17/17 by N. Layne, N. Parker, S. Reiter, S Grey & R. McNeil. Properties include Trump Hollywood, 2711 S. Ocean Dr., 13 Units; Sunny Isles Beach, Trump Grande, 18201 Collins Ave. 27 Units. 18101 Collins Ave, 16 Units, 18001 Collins Ave, 1 unit, Trump Towers, 16001 Collins Ave .,5 units, 15901 Collins Ave, 8 units, 15811 Collins Ave, 7 units.

According to McClatchy. 2/27/17, G. Garvin, Trump sold a Palm Beach Mansion at 515 N. County Rd, to a Russian for $95 million, for which Trump paid $41.35 million.

From Russia to New York.

Bloomberg Businessweek, on line 3/15/17, Trump World Tower, 845 United Nations Plaza, tallest residential building in the U.S. at 90 stories has several million in private Russian investments, by M. Smith, A. Sazanov & P Mosendz.

According to Business Insider, 5/17/17, N. Bertrand, Russia State Bank VEB helped refinance Trump's Toronto Hotel.

Donald Trump had Russian money on his mind since 1987, when he met Mikhail S. Gorbachev. He planned a shopping mall with Moscow Mayor, Yuri M. Luzhkov. Wikipedia, *Business Projects of Donald Trump in Russia*, citing Twohey, Megan; Eder, Steve (January 16, 2017), 'For Trump. Three Decades of Chasing Deals in Russia', New York Times; Belton, Catherine; Stott, Michael (December 13, 2016), 'Trump's Russian Connections', Financial Times ,London.

Appendix 2

PUTIN TRUMP TIMELINE

1991 Trump Taj Mahal filed bankruptcy

1992 Trump Castle Associates filed bankruptcy

1996 Bill Browder takes Hermitage Capital to Russia.

1999 Putin saves Yeltsin & frames Prosecutor Yuri Skuratov to stop probe.

1999 Yeltsin impressed with Putin, makes him President of Russia.

2004 Trump Hotels and Casino Resorts Inc. filed bankruptcy.

2006 Putin blacklists Browder for charging Gazprom executives with fraud.

2007 Putin mobsters raid Hermitage, defraud Russia of $230 mm in taxes.

June 2007 Putin convicts Magnitsky of fraud that *Magnitsky uncovered*.

11/16/09 Sergei Magnitsky died mysteriously in custody in prison at age 37.

2009 Trump Entertainment Resorts filed bankruptcy.

2011 Trump becomes Birther in Chief, denying President Obama's birth in Hawaii.

8/29/11 Rosneft awards Exxon Mobil a large contract.

12/6/2012 U.S. passes Magnitsky Act to sanction Russian officials personally.

12/28/12 Retaliating for Magnitsky act, Putin bans Americans from adoption.

2012-2014 Paul Manafort advises President Yanukovych, Putin's man in Ukraine.

6/8/13 Trump tweets: Will Putin go to Miss Universe Contest?

2013 Trump takes Miss Universe Pageant to Moscow, deals with Aras Agaralov.

5/23/14 Russia's Rosneft Oil signs another agreement with Exxon Mobil.

2014 Ukraine overthrows Yanukovych regime. Russia invades Crimea.

2014 President Obama imposes sanctions on Russia for Ukraine invasion.

July 2015 Russians start hacking DNC computers.

2015 Trump enters GOP Primaries.

7/2015 GRU Russia Military Intelligence accessed DNC Computers.

9/2015 FBI Agent A. Hawkins warns DNC of Russian hacking.

12/2015 Russia Social Media starts to advocate for Trump's election.

12/10/15 Lt. Gen (Ret.) Michael Flynn speaks at Russia RT conference.

2/1/16 Trump places second to Ted Cruz in Iowa Caucuses.

2/26/16 Flynn joins Trump. Senator Jeff Sessions endorses Trump.

3/19/16 Phishing email to John Podesta: *"Someone has your password"*.

3/21/16 Trump lists foreign advisers, including Carter Page.

3/29/16 Trump announced Paul Manafort as Campaign Manager.

4/27/16 Trump policy speech at Mayflower Hotel, will work with Russia.

6/3/16 Rob Goldstone emails Don, Jr., Russia supports Trump.

6/6/16 Goldstone emails. Emin Agaralov wants Don to meet Veselnitskaya.

6/14/16 Washington Post reported that Russians hacked DNC computers.

6/716 Trump promises misdeeds speech on Hillary Clinton next week.

6/9/16 Don, Jr., Manafort, Kushner meet Natalia Veselnitskaya.

7/18/16 Campaign removes anti-Russia sanctions plank from Platform.

7/22/16 WikiLeaks dumps 20,000 DNC emails.

7/24/16 Debbie Wassermann Schulz resigned as DNC Chair.

10/7/16 HLS & DNI confident Russia behind email hacks.

6/16 to 7/17 Team Trump denies any meetings with Russians.

7/12/17 Team Trump dribbles out details of Veselnitskaya meeting.

10/7/16 HLS & DNI confident that Russia hacked emails.

11/08/16 Donald trump wins the 2016 presidential election.

12/29/16 Pres. Obama orders new sanctions against Russia for interference.

12/30/16 Trump praises Putin for not retaliating against expulsion.

1/11/17 Trump denies Russia contacts. Denies allegations in Dossier.

1/20/17 President Trump inaugurated.

Jan-Mar 2017 Sessions, Flynn, & Kushner omit Russian contacts from SF86.

1/26/17 Acting AG Sally Yates reports that Flynn is a risk.

2/12/17 Lt. Gen (Ret.) Michael Flynn resigns.

5/9/17 President Trump dismisses FBI Director James Comey.

5/17/17 Deputy AG Rosenstein appointed Special Counsel Robert Mueller

7/12/17 Don Jr. dribbles out meeting with Veselnitskaya.

7/13/17 President T rump said, *'Most people would have taken the meeting.'*